Wickford

memories

Jim Reeve

TEMPUS

Frontispiece: Wickford Garden Village. (Copyright Basildon Council)

First published 2005

Tempus Publishing Limited
The Mill, Brimscombe Port,
Stroud, Gloucestershire, GL5 2QG

© Jim Reeve, 2005

British Library Cataloguing in Publication Data.
A catalogue record for this book is available from the British Library.

ISBN 0 7524 3558 2

Typesetting and origination by Tempus Publishing Limited
Printed in Great Britain

Wickford
memories

WICKFORD

Southend Rd.

HIGH ST.

The Garden Village Estate

Country Homes for Health Seekers.

Freehold Land for Investment.

THE LAND COMPANY, 68, CHEAPSIDE, LONDON, E.C.

Contents

Acknowledgements 6

Introduction 7

one Early Days 9

two Preparing for Life 21

three Wickford Market 37

four Wickford at Work 43

five Flooding 61

six Wickford at Play 69

seven Wickford in Uniform 93

eight Transport 119

nine Famous and Infamous People of Wickford 125

Acknowledgements

I would like to thank the many people who have assisted me in compiling this book and have generously given me their time, shared their life experiences and loaned me their precious photographs. I would especially like to thank Jo Cullum at Wickford Library for her help and knowledge; the Café in the Square for introducing me to the first person my wife and I interviewed; Mrs Cockie (Miss Amos) for so many interesting introductions; Barrie Adcock and Peter Hall, whose records and history of Wickford have to be seen to be believed; and to Yvonne Abbott, Emily Babbage, Mr Barker, Mrs Barker, Joan Blackburn, Carl Beck, Joan Cox, Mrs Dines, John Dowman, Val Dowman, Christine Hoad (*née* Franklin), Alan Goddard, Stan Gregory, Roy Hall, Beryl Humprey, Reg Iles, Jackie Joyce, Mrs Livermore, William Mead, Mr Nightingale, Eddie Noyes, Doris Orton, Barbara Pocock, Pat and Charles Read, Doreen Reed, Mr and Mrs Reeves, Norman and Phyllis Simmons, Fred Smith, Mr Spindler, Queenie Thorington, Joyce and Ken Ward, Yvonne Wilkinson, Doreen Williams, Mr Williams Senior, Trevor Williams and Ernie Woods. I have, where it is known, obtained permission for the copyright of the many photographs that I have used. I would especially like to thank Basildon District Council for allowing me to use their photographs of Wickford. I have taken every care in setting out details and facts as related to me and any omissions or mistakes in the project are mine; I apologise in advance and hope you will forgive me.

I would like to say a special thank you to my younger son, Paul, for scanning and transferring the photographs on to a CD and for all his help, and to my elder son Stephan for his support and advice. Finally my wife, Joan, who accompanied me on most of the interviews and edited the book before submission and without whose help, patience and understanding this project would never have been completed.

Flooding in Wickford, 1947

Introduction

Wickford has fascinated me since childhood when, during the Second World War, my grandfather used to bring me to the market from Rawreth to buy a dozen day-old chicks, out of which, if he was lucky, one would survive. We would wander through the animal market, I hanging on to his coat-tails trying not to get lost among the milling crowd while I took in the sights, smells and noises of the cattle, sheep and pigs. Once my grandfather had made his purchases, he would adjourn to the Castle public house so that he could slake his thirst with his favourite drink, a pint of mild and bitter, while I had a long wait on the step outside. If I was lucky, I would get a lemonade but I loved to sit on the doorstep, observing the many characters that passed through the door, some ruffling my hair as they went. When my grandfather had drunk his fill, I would follow in his unsteady wake down to the bus stop. I remember well the bumpy, twisting ride back to the Carpenters' Arms public house. Often I would accompany my mother into Wickford for shopping and sometimes, as a treat, the cinema, which used to fire my imagination and I would walk around for weeks pretending to be the hero of the film.

I have endeavoured to capture some of the voices of Wickford, to give a glimpse of the past from residents who have lived through the vast changes that have taken place since the birth of the last century. People like Queenie Thorington, who has lived through all the changes and who remembers the Zeppelin flying over Wickford and her parents taking her to Great Burstead to see its remains after it had been shot out of the sky by Fl. Lt Sowrey and Fl. Lt Robinson; Mrs Cockie (Miss Amos), who taught generations of Wickford's children for over forty years; and Mr Spindler, whose ship was chased by a submarine during the Second World War. If these moments of ordinary people's lives are not recorded, they will be lost for ever.

Wickford is a thriving town. In 1901 the population was 638 and it has climbed steadily to its present level of 27,000. Four main factors have contributed to the changes and population growth seen by the town: the railway, the plotlands, the Second World War and being swallowed by Basildon. It was evident by the 1880s that Wickford needed a railway: goods for the town had to be unloaded at Pitsea, Chelmsford or Shenfield and transported by road to Wickford, which added to the costs and led to dearer prices. With public opinion clamouring for the railway to be extended, Parliament passed an Act in 1883 enabling the Great Eastern Railway to build a line from Shenfield to Southend, passing through Wickford, and the first goods train stopped at Wickford station in 1888. It was not until three months later that the first passenger train steamed into the station and took on board two ladies and a policeman.

The plotlands were an idea to help farmers in financial difficulties; the railway line helped many farmers but for those who grew grain it was too late as it was now being imported cheaply from America and Canada. In 1891, the Land Company came to their rescue by buying up farmland, dividing it into plots and advertising it for sale in London. They ran special trains from London to Wickford, Billericay and Laindon, where a fleet of carriages took the prospective buyers out to the farms. Once purchased, many plots lay unused and lead to land disputes in later years. However, some owners made good use of them and came down to camp on their land at weekends, in school holidays and for whole summers. Many owners gradually built shacks, which over the years were transformed into the very desirable dwellings of today.

During the Second World War, many people came to Wickford to escape the bombing in London. A large number moved on to the plots that had been purchased at the latter end of the nineteenth century. Many of these refugees stayed after the hostilities finished, having found that the tranquillity and clean air of a small town suited them.

After the Second World War, a lot of London lay in ruins and the Government embarked on a massive building scheme. Under the New Towns Act of 1946, a number of areas throughout the country were designated for the building of New Towns, Basildon being one of them. Much of the area was still shrubland with unmade roads and although many occupiers of the plotlands had built beautiful buildings, most were still shacks with no running water or sanitary arrangements. At this time Wickford and the surrounding district came under the local government of Billericay and Chelmsford but once Basildon was designated as a New Town and it started to flex its muscles it was not long before it grew and became the dominant partner, taking Billericay and part of Wickford under its wing. With Basildon Development Corporation's vast building programme of houses and factories, many firms – like Ford, Ilford and STC – transferred to these cheaper premises with the added bonus of good accommodation for their employees. London Boroughs began to reduce their housing waiting lists. At first it was necessary to be sponsored by the firm but in later years this was waived. During the 1970s, 16 per cent of the tenants transferring to Basildon came to one of the estates in Wickford.

I find it difficult to understand some people's observations that Wickford is just a dormitory town that lacks community spirit. Admittedly, a large number of people do work in London and travel up each day but of the sixty people I interviewed while compiling this book, only five had worked in London. With regard to community spirit, what of the Community Hall – built partly by public subscription – and its many activities: dancing, chess, fencing, keep fit and, of course, the bar? What of the Horticultural Society, the British Legion, the cricket and tennis clubs, the swimming pool, the Writing Circle, the excellent library and the different churches? Many people will say that these are for the older generation, but for the younger generation there are the Scouts, the Guides, the Air Training Corps and many more!

I have found Wickford a friendly, thriving place which, although it has changed much since my visits to the market with my grandfather, is still a good place to live!

Jim Reeve
March, 2005

one

Early Days

Above: A typical plotland dwelling.

Below: Land for sale. (Copyright Basildon Council)

One of the first

In the 1890s, my grandfather, Henry William Iles, used to hire trains to bring people down from London and take them out to the farms where they would buy the plots. It was a real day out.

Reg Iles

Granny Fletcher

Granny Fletcher was well into her nineties and wore long dresses, boots which she did up with a buttonhook and her grey hair was pulled back in a bow. We would visit her every Sunday morning and if we had anything new on we had to show her. She would say, 'Those shoes look nice, how much were they and where did your mother get them?' She would ask us the price right down to our socks. She had this great big parrot, Laura, and when you walked in it would say 'Hello'.

Doris Orton

Just mud tracks

The roads were just mud tracks with grass growing out of them. A lot of the roads were marked out with wire and posts and I think they intended to do them but the First World War came along and put a stop to the improvement. It was like that until the 1920s. Across Station Road were the plotlands where people had bought pieces of land and built little shacks. They were like that until quite recently when they were extended or rebuilt.

Queenie Thorington

The conversion

We were bombed out of Canning Town in 1940. At first we moved to Wiltshire, until 1942 when we came to Wickford. The house was originally a cowshed, which I think was converted in 1920. Beside mum and dad there was my brother and me. We had no mains drainage but we did have electricity. My dad was in the building trade.

Stan Gregory

Burnt sausages

We came to Wickford in 1957 because of burnt sausages. When I was eleven, I went camping at Whitewebbs Park with the Edmonton Girl Guides, where we burnt the sausages. When I got home I said to my father, 'Can't we buy a bit of land to put a tent on?' My father looked in the *Exchange and Mart* and saw some land in Billericay for sale and to satisfy me we looked at it. It was covered in brambles. He shook his head and said, 'I'm not spending my weekends clearing that just for you to put a tent on.' I was really upset. Then we drove into Wickford and spotted a notice in the window of this little toy shop opposite where Woolworths is now. It said 'Weekend Chalet for Sale'. Dad shook hands on the deal for £150 and that was it. It was in Canford Avenue and was

Mrs Thorington's grandfather, William, with Tyke.

called St David's. When I was seventeen, we moved into a bungalow, in the same road, called Bobill.

Joyce Ward

Summer holidays

I was born in Rotherhithe on 31 May 1922, opposite the Surrey Commercial Docks. My father had a coffee shop and his customers came straight off the boats. I don't know where my grandfather was born but he had a farm called Frierns on London Road in Wickford. Each Thursday, he and my grandmother would go up to their fish business in Upton Park, London to serve their Jewish customers in the Queens Road market. The fish were sold straight out of the box with their heads on or the customers would not buy them. When my twin and I were eight, we started staying with our grandparents in Wickford for the summer holidays. Grandfather was very strict and at mealtimes he made us sit down to eat. At dinner, my grandparents drank wine and we had water. We could not get up until everybody had finished. Grandfather smoked only cigars, drank at home and on market days never went into the Castle public house with the other farmers. He would give us a penny and say, 'You play ball out here while I work in the dairy.' Occasionally he would take us down to Southend to walk the length of the pier and back. In those days, the summers were long and beautiful but a month is a long time when you are a child and I used to get homesick.

Doris Orton

Milk in churns

During the war, when I was four years old, we came down to a bungalow in Wickford to get away from the bombing in Woodford. A man called Eggie collected us from the station in his cart and took us to a bungalow right out in the wilds. It had a veranda and we used to pretend it was our boat. We would wash in cold water from the well in the garden. For lighting we used oil lamps. We loved it. The milkman used to call with a big churn of milk and would fill our jugs from it.

Joan Blackburn

Fireworks

I was born in The Almonds in London Road. I should have been born on 25 November 1937 but my mother went to a fireworks display, a rocket went up and she went into labour. Wickford used to be a lovely little village in those days. My father, Kenneth William Adcock, was born in Ipswich and came to Wickford in 1935 and started up a business. He bought a draper's shop in Moulsham

An old cottage on a site next to where Woolworths is today, turn of the twentieth century.

two

Preparing for Life

Mothers and fathers

I was eight in 1918. My younger sister, my cousin and her brother used to play mothers and fathers. We had a little place in the hedge away from the house. We used to make big rooms and a kitchen in it. We got pieces of broken cups, saucers and plates, and saucepans with no handles. We would say to the two young ones, 'Go out and get the dinner.' They would go and gather blackberries, hips, wild strawberries and pansies, they were only tiny little things but we would pick them. We would eat all sorts of things but we never got poisoned. My cousin came recently and we talked about the big ash tree and how its roots stuck out of the ground.

The only thing that came up the unmade muddy paths in winter was the coal cart pulled by horses and they left deep ruts in the ground. It was all horses in those days. There were special low farm carts which were low so that they could be easily loaded. The milk cart had their measures hanging on the side. Mum would take the milk jug out to the farmer for him to fill. We also had bread delivered by a pony and trap which had big wheels. We had a good healthy diet. At weekends, we had an H-bone and Yorkshires, sometimes we would have suet pudding for sweet or spotted dick with custard. All through the Second World War, my husband grew all our vegetables and we had loads of fruit off the trees: apples, pears and plums.

Queenie Thorington

Another world

The Wick used to be a farm. One of the farms belonged to a friend of ours and when we walked across the level crossing at Wick Lane it was like going to another world.

Yvonne Wilkinson

I was born on washday

I was born on a washday in 1929 on Does Hill Farm, which was my grandfather's. He had been captain on a barge but always wanted to be a farmer and so when he had saved enough money he bought the farm. It was mainly a dairy farm and I used to go with him on his milk round when I was three. The toilet was down the garden. There was no electricity so Mum cooked on an oil stove. The electric was not laid on until 1949. Mum did the washing by hand and boiled it up in a copper.

Shirley Dines

A twist of fate

My grandfather Archer had cancer and was advised to get out of London and so he started to look round for somewhere in the country to live and heard of Bridge House Farm going for sale in Wickford. He got off the train in 1890 and started off for the farm in a pony and trap. He instructed the driver, 'The road on the left' but he took the wrong road and came up this road, Church Road, instead of going up the Southend Road. It was then that Grandfather saw the 'For Sale' sign on Shotgate Farm and noticed the cottage across the road was included so he bought them for £900. He knew nothing about farming and learnt as he went along. My dad lived in the cottage while my aunt and two uncles lived in the farmhouse.

When Grandad was eighteen, he walked from Cornwall to London looking for work. He got married and finished up with three pubs; one, the Coach and Horses, was in Homerton, Hackney. There was the Adam and Eve and a third one, the name of which I cannot remember. I think the third pub was near the docks and passengers would come off the boats straight into the pub.

I was born on the farm in 1920 and brought up here. We had to collect water from the well which was the other side of the kitchen. It is now bricked over. The toilet was a long wooden building with three seats in it: dad's, mum's and child's. Dad had to empty it out; we had the best rhubarb you have ever seen. We are still not on the mains sewerage and have a septic tank.

None of my dad's sisters married. Aunty Alice's boyfriend came home on leave from the First World War, did some painting on the farm, went back and was killed. She never married. My Aunt Mary was an Assistant Matron at Rochford Hospital, they called them Night Superintendents then and nurses never married. My dad was the only one who married and I was the only child. Aunty Alice would have made a wonderful teacher. She taught me everything and we used to go up to Rawreth church to clean the brass, wash the linen and do the flowers. She taught me how to kill, pluck and draw the chickens. We never bought eggs and had a big vegetable garden in which we grew all our own vegetables. The Carters built the cowsheds for our eighteen cows, who all had names. We did grow some corn and potatoes. We had a couple of big horses who did the ploughing but we had one of the first tractors. As kids, we used to swim in the river at the Joinings. We would come home smothered in mud but in the 1950s they had a case of polio and we stopped using it.

Joan Cox

Joan Cox's father, Mr Archer, contemplating the world at Shotgate.

Joan Cox at the age of twenty.

Daisy

We had dolls and teddy bears. My doll had hair and eyes that opened and shut. She was not very big. My dad suggested I called her Daisy after my mother. Mum made her lots of clothes. One of my uncles knocked all her teeth out when he pushed a cigarette in her mouth. I never forgave him.

Queenie Thorington

Opening of the arterial road

I was born in Wickford in 1922 and lived at Hovefields House, Hovefields Avenue. Everybody was friendly, our postmen were Fred White and Fred Garland and came from Wickford families. Hovefields Avenue was an unmade road and we would repair it with stones and hoggin bought from F.A. Norton & Son with money that was collected from some of the residents. Before 1924, when the first, southern lane of the Arterial Road (A127) was built, Hovefields Avenue was not cut in two. I don't remember that happening but at two years of age I remember waving a flag at the opening of the Arterial Road as one of the King and Queen's sons went by. I lived in the house until I was called up in 1942. Hovefields Avenue was a fantastic place to live and the people were great. We had about two acres of garden, orchard and lawns including a tennis court. It's all now covered by a large warehouse and marked Hovefields Court. Before I got called up, I was a Local Defence Volunteer, which became known as the Home Guard.

Reg Iles

On the move

I was born in Rochford Hospital and lived in one of the red-brick Hayes Cottages in Woodham Road. We moved to Shot Farm, Shotgate and then after a few years Father put a few sticks up on the horse and cart and we trotted over to Chichester Farm.

Ernie Woods

The Memorial Gates

The Memorial Gates in Runwell Road were put up in memory of Mr Haddon, who did a lot for Wickford cricket club. I was vice-president for a while. Wickford was a village in those days and we all knew one another. As a kid, I used to go haymaking with the people in Long Meadow Drive, which is up the Southend Road. I think that one farm was the Keelings', who owned machines and hired them out. He did sell them to an Australian firm but regretted it when they melted them down. As schoolboys, they only used to pay us fourpence. I used to earn a bob or two from an old chap called Mr Ruth, who owned the old ironmonger's in Southend Road. He used to recharge accumulator batteries. I would collect them for a halfpenny one Saturday and take them back the next.

Barrie Adcock

Born over the chemist shop

I was born over the top of the chemist's in Wickford High Street and then we moved to Woolshots Road. Unfortunately, when I was five and a half years old in 1937 my mother died and I got shunted around between grand-parents, aunts and uncles. I finished up in Elm Road, Wickford, opposite the cricket ground. I lived there for twenty years until I got married in 1956 to Valerie, known to everybody as Val. Wickford in those days was a much quieter and nicer place. I would go shopping in the High Street for my aunt, who would give me sixpence.

John Dowman

One of the teachers terrified me

I started school in Wickford in January 1935, when it was all one school which is the one situated near the library. One of the teachers terrified me and my older brother and sister, and any time I was left alone I was down the corridor and out the door. When you had finished a book, you had to take it up to his room. He was always looking for an excuse to cane you and would have it by his side all the time. If you had made a blot or had not used all the pages, you were in for it. I never got it. The school later became the junior school and when the war came I went to the church school in Southend Road. I enjoyed it there. When the Battle of Britain was raging, we spent a lot of time in the air-raid shelter. It is surprising to me how we ever learnt anything. We were each allocated a senior to keep us safe. Somebody opened a private school in Park Drive, which only had five pupils and only did two hours a day. My education started slipping and in the end I went back to Wickford School and soon caught up.

Shirley Dines

Mrs Dines at Mrs Cockie's (Miss Amos') quarterly reunion of her 1942 class.

Birdnesting

When I was at school, we had a headmaster who was very strict and would cane you for anything. I was petrified of him. There used to be a line of elms and in those days nobody thought it was wrong to take bird's eggs. I took an egg from a mistle thrush's nest. In those days all the kids went birdnesting.

John Dowman

Top to tail

There were seven children and we slept top to tail. My brothers would get under our bed in the night and lift it and we would call mum. We had a great childhood and would play a game called 'All on top'. If somebody fell on the floor, we would shout out, 'All on top!' and we would all pile on one another. We were not allowed to swear, say 'Liar' or to sing one of the popular songs of the day, 'Oh, You Rotten Liar', and so we hummed it . We played games like lying in bed and see who could whistle the longest without laughing. As there were no cars in Highcliff Road, we played whip-and-top, knock down ginger, tin can tommy and hopscotch in the middle of the road. The town has gradually changed. The High Road remained the same for a long while but it did get congested. Before they put a pavement in by the side of the railway bridge, you had to take your life in your hands by walking in the middle of the road. As kids, we would build camps in the ground and cover them with corrugated sheeting, put branches on top and then dig a tunnel for the entrance. We would play for hours.

Mrs Livermore

Sunday school

On Sunday afternoons, we were all sent to Sunday school so that mum and dad had some time alone. We were always being chucked out of the various churches, the Salvation Army, the Congregational, the Church of England and the Methodist. Most of the churches ran some clubs. My sister and I went to the Girls' Life Brigade but got thrown out. We joined the Methodist church and sang in the choir but got the giggles and got chucked out. When one of the local vicars left, I went and sang to him. When the Methodist church shut, we broke in and climbed right to the top to play the organ. The church was in the Southend Road but it has gone now.

Mrs Livermore

One of the first women vicars

Canon Christine McCatherty took over St Catherine's from Roy Thomas. She was one of the first women vicars in the country. At first I objected to having a woman vicar but she soon won me round. She looked after three churches, St Mary's, St Catherine's and St Andrew's. She was the senior rector and had vicars working for her. She has gone to Little Baddow now and spends a lot of time at Chelmsford Cathedral. I take the Edward Bear Club at St Catherine's church. It is for mums and toddlers. There is also a youth club for youngsters of fourteen to about sixteen. St Catherine's is a good church with a warm atmosphere.

Phyllis Simmons

St Catherine's church.

The road was one big green tunnel

We moved to Crays Hill by accident. We lived in Kent and STC [Standard Telephones and Cables] were moving to Basildon and the toll through the new Dartford Tunnel was going to be 2s 6d. One wet Saturday afternoon in February 1964, I was unable to play hockey, West Ham were playing away and so I said to my wife, 'Let's go house-hunting.' We finished up in an estate agent's in Billericay with a list of houses in our hands. We came to this one and it was the only one we liked. The London Road was just a green tunnel and lined with elm trees on each side. It was sad when all the trees got Dutch elm disease. I had to take three trees down in my garden, sawing them by hand while looking down on the roofs of the double-decker buses.

There were many pre-war wooden shacks here and a little sweet shop on the corner but they have all gone now.

Pat and Charles Read

School during the First World War

I started school during the First World War. We had Mr Hearn, who was very strict and gave the boys the cane even if they misbehaved going home because he said they were still under his control. The girls never got caned. They used to have mixed classes but they were segregated for some lessons, like needlework and cookery. The boys did woodwork. Every other week, we would march down the street from our school down the Southend Road

Wickford girls' class, 1947.

up Market Road to what we called the New School, where we took cookery. It is now an infants' school. In the playground, the boys played football with a tennis ball and the girls played rounders, skipping and hoops. As there was hardly any traffic, we would bowl our wooden hoops all along the centre of the road with our sticks. The boys had iron hoops with what they called a skimmer, which was a hook, and by some magic they would keep them going for ages. I longed for one. Another game was tops, which we kept going with a whip all along the road. When our whips got tatty, my cousin and I got the bright idea of asking men if they had any string, most men in those days were like Boy Scouts, they carried string, a penknife, a pencil and a shilling. Night after night, we would stop all the men. They got so used to us doing it that directly they saw us they would jump off their bikes and start searching their pockets. We collected big balls of it

and put it in pots. Getting the string became more interesting than spinning the top. I stayed in the same school until I was fourteen then I left for work.

Queenie Thorington

A taste for music

I used to play the music for the nativity play every year. There was one boy I remember who played Joseph, I think he now runs the bicycle shop at the end of the town. What my pupils remembered was the music appreciation lessons. I have been told by old men of seventy to whom I taught music that they still like listening to classical music. One chap said, 'I still love listening to *The Sorcerer's Apprentice* and Benjamin Britten's *A Young Person's Guide to the Orchestra.*' Once they started to like it, you could then move on and show them how a symphony was put together.

Mary Cockie (Miss Amos)

Joan Blackburn with Mary Cockie today.

Only two schools

When I was young, there were only two schools in Wickford, a junior and a senior. I went to the senior school just to get a certificate so I could leave.

Emily Babbage

School favourites

Until I was eleven, I went to the church school in Wickford. Mr Bullock was our headmaster and my friend Anne and I were his favourites. The school had no central heating but he had a pot-bellied stove which he was glued to. He was just like an old grandad. Then I went to Wickford Secondary School, which is now the junior school, at the end of the market.

Yvonne Wilkinson

Chip loaf

Mum would give us our dinner money and instead of getting lunch we would buy a crusty loaf, rip the middle out and stuff it full of chips. We called that a chip loaf. When I was about twelve, my brother Douglas and Billy Brown and his mates used to race on bikes on a speed track. The Rayleigh Rockets would come down on their motorbikes for the races. We used to race other clubs from all over. We had a gang called the Shotgate Boys. Peter Smith and his mate from Woodham Ferrers were part of it. We used to hang around Shotgate on motorbikes and years later when I met him I hardly recognised him. He was bald! As kids, we went scrumping over the orchard by the A127. We took off our jumpers and filled them up with apples and when the farmer came we ran like hell, normally dropping all we had picked. We made our own spears by flattening pieces of metal on the railway and fitting them in the end of a stick. We also put pennies on the railway lines to flatten them out. We used to go to the Saturday Morning Pictures in the old Salvation Hall and watch films like *Tom Mix*. We used to have drinks with straws and would blow

Dirt track racing, from left to right: Doug Smith, Ron Ball, Douggie Rowland, Buntman Wallman, Jimmy Brown, Billy Thorn.

through the straw and send the cartons flying down the front. The Alfresco café was in the Southend Road and we used to play the old record machines.

Fred Smith

You dared not answer back

If a teacher told you to do something, you did it. You never answered back, especially if it was Mr Fountain, who used a ruler and threw bits of chalk at the boys. He did not do it to the girls though. All the boys that played up were put down the front. Mr Gash was my form teacher and his wife, Mrs Gash, took us girls for domestic science. Miss Amos took us for religious instruction and music. The school used to bus some kids in from Woodham Ferrers. My husband went to the same school but I did not know him there because the school was so big.

Mrs Barker

My husband left school at thirteen

My husband went to a school in Rettendon which had an allotment. The teacher not only got the boys to dig that but also his own garden. When his grandfather found out he said, 'If I'd known he was doing that at school he could have stopped at home and done mine.' He left school when he was thirteen.

Queenie Thorington

Sports in all weathers

We played football in winter and cricket in summer. The girls played netball and hockey. We had quite a good football team. Mr Ross was the PE teacher and we went out in all weathers, snow, rain, just in shorts and a little vest. It was freezing. The girls were treated the same. At the senior school, Mr Crook was the woodwork teacher. Mr Fountain was the

science teacher and Mr Gash the rural science teacher. He was very strict. We had vegetable plots in the grounds and Mr Gash was looking out of the window one day and called me over because he thought I was talking and I got the cane, one on each hand. I went to school in Market Road, which was the juniors and seniors. I remember going to school with my gas mask in its box and the drinking chocolate which I think came from America. We had milk each day. The teachers at the junior were really good and the ones I remember were Miss Saltwell – who used to arrive at school in her little Austin Seven – and Mrs Mason the art teacher. There was also a Mrs Brewster who lived at the bottom of Irvon Hill and a Mrs Andrews. At the senior school, the teachers were Mr Crook, Miss Amos the music teacher and Mrs Riggs, who came from Rettendon and took the remedial class.

Stan Gregory

The scholarship

My sister did not want to go to the church school without me and so she played up. As a result, I was allowed to start before I was of school age. My mum always encouraged me to do well. She used to say to me 'If you pass the scholarship, I'll buy you something.' I did pass and went to Rayleigh Technical School, where I met my husband. My mum was so proud that I had passed and one day she told the bus conductor that I was going to take an oral examination. I was so embarrassed. What passing the scholarship meant in those days was you either became a teacher or a secretary. I became a secretary and never looked back and I've never been without a job. You did not have the options that girls have today. You could not change courses halfway through. My greatest ambition was to become a PE teacher. I used to do a lot of running and netball but because my father had died of TB my mother was frightened that I was not strong enough but I was. I worked up in London for a long while and I finished up working at Ford's.

Mrs Livermore

Church of England infants' school

I've got two daughters and they went to the Church of England Infants School in the Southend Road and then to the Wickford Junior School, which at the time was into music. They used to have concerts there every year but not any more.

Eddie Noyes

A bit of all right

I started school at Rawreth. The teacher I remember was Mrs Hodson. She was nice. She lived in a little thatched bungalow. There were two teachers and two little classrooms. My brother went back to Rawreth School for an open day many years later and said 'I've seen your name in the book. You had two strokes of the cane, didn't you?' I replied, 'That's nothing to be proud of because you did as well!' The secret was to hold your hand down so that the cane slipped off but then they hit you across the wrist and that hurt. I was at that school until I was eleven and then I went to Wickford Senior School.

Ernie Woods

Beauchamps was a poultry farm

I went to nearly every school in Wickford except Beauchamps and that used to be a poultry farm until they made it into a school. When we were at woodwork, we would take

Rawreth School, 2005.

a bit of tobacco in with us and we'd ask Mr Crook for a paper to roll a fag. He didn't like it. We played spinning tops and hopscotch. I was bought a yo-yo when I was fourteen and I have still got it. I remember some of the teachers, particularly Mr Gash. He was the gardening teacher and was a bit of a disciplinarian. Mr Lovelock, he was also a bit of a disciplinarian. When I was twelve, jeans came out but the teachers did not like them and picked on us. I was sitting in class and Mr Gash picked me out and said, 'Smith, spell chrysanthemum' and I sniffed. I got a right whacking for that. I got hit on the head with a book. Miss Hope, we used to call her 'No Hope' in fun. We used to throw the old pens like darts. I learnt more from life after I left school.

Fred Smith

Fires at the old church school

I went to the old church school in Southend Road and it caught fire three times. They used to heat the dinners on the gas and somebody must have left it on and up it went. It was a lovely school. I liked the headmaster, Mr Bullock, and I remember him walking down from his home in the early morning to the school and he would have his paper under his arm. As soon as he got to the school gate he would say, 'Good morning, boys. Good morning, girls.' There was a Miss Jones, who was a really nice person who used to live in The Grange, which is now a residential home. When I left that school, I went to a private one in Southend called Westminster College. I used to travel down there on the No. 151 or No. 152 at 7.30 every morning.

Barrie Adcock

Teachers are not always right

At the church open day, an old school register caught my eye. It read 'This child called the headmaster a blockhead and he will never do well or amount to anything.' They were talking about my brother who, despite their predictions, is a very successful businessman. Another entry said 'Terrence Hutton was sent home because he had hurt his hand and had to keep it in his pocket. My brother laughed when I showed him a copy of the entry. What the headmaster didn't know was that he'd kept his hand in his pocket because he had a frog in it. We lived in Shotgate and Mum could not afford the penny fares for five of us to go on the bus to Wickford School and so we walked, we walked everywhere.

Yvonne Wilkinson

Wickford Church School

I started to teach at Hutton Residential School. The pupils mainly lived in but we did have a few day students. They came to us via the courts, not that they had done anything wrong, it was their parents. Some had their mothers with them. I then obtained a post at Wickford Church School and became head. Teaching in those days was good fun. We taught infants. The Church took a great interest. I left teaching when I had my children but returned later to do some supply teaching with children who had learning difficulties. I then took a degree in maths and finished up coaching children for their GCEs. I got a lot of pleasure from seeing them pass their exams and going to university.

Phyllis Simmons

My teacher, Miss Amos

I started school during the Second World War and immediately we noticed the difference as the men joined up. Very few children passed the examination for high school as we had missed so much school because of the raids. When I went to senior school, it took me a

Teachers at Wickford School, 1953. From left to right, front row: Miss Evans, Mrs Gash, Miss McCarthy, Mrs Gray, Mrs Roebuck, Mrs Rose, Mrs Cockie, Miss Spencer. Middle row: Mr Brooks, Mr Miller, Mr Fountain, Mr Rose (headmaster), Mr Phillips, Mr Richards, Mr Ryman, Mr Lovelock. Back row: Mr Fountain, Mr Gash, Mr Ross, Mr Hibbs, -?-.

year to catch up. Our first-year teacher was Miss Amos, who was very young and played the piano beautifully and had the ability to make lessons fun. I think she took us for maths and English, but the other subjects – history, geography, games, needlework and cookery – were taken by specialists. By the second year, I had regained all the confidence I had lost in the junior school. Mr Mason was our second-year teacher and we sat an examination to see if we qualified for the Mid-Essex Technical School in Chelmsford. I passed but before I left I was introduced to sewing gar-

ments and embroidery by Mrs Mason. You had to have coupons for cloth and so we made all the garments from old ones. Men's trousers were unpicked and made into ladies' skirts, shirts were made into blouses. Nothing was wasted. We made do and mended. New clothes were an exciting event. We even had to give coupons for our new school uniforms. All we were allowed was one of everything. During the war, we had very few trips; in fact I can remember only one and that was when we travelled to Whipsnade Zoo. We all packed in my father's van and enjoyed a day of animals and a picnic. Other than that, we found our fun walking over the fields by the River Crouch.

Christine Hoad (née Franklin)

Rebellion

I remember coming home from school in the lunch break and saying, 'I've had enough. I don't want to go back to school,' and my mum chasing me back. I left school at fourteen. The teachers I remember were Mrs Mason, Mrs Roebuck, Mrs Weston and Mr Crook the carpenter, who took both the boys and girls for woodwork and cookery. We only cooked cakes as everything was on ration. At woodwork I made a wooden heart and when we got married my dad had the heart put on our photos. Miss Amos, now Mrs Cockie, was a really good teacher. She played the piano and we sang to it. I was surprised to find that when my boys went to school she was still there.

Mrs Reeves

Double top

I remember that we used to break the nibs of pens to make darts and make ink pellets out of blotting paper and ping them up to the ceiling with rulers.

John Dowman

The cane

I went to Wickford Senior School and was in 2A, Miss Atkins' class. She married the

Mr and Mrs Reeves today.

Mrs Cockie, front row, centre, with an early class.

art teacher, Mr Mason. We had a very good headmaster called Mr Rose. In those days, if you did something wrong you got the cane and they recorded it in the register. Once I was in the queue and somebody pushed me so I shoved them back and got the cane. Mr Ross was the PT instructor. They were good, happy days despite having to walk a mile and a quarter to school and back again for dinner. In 1939 the war started and the teachers got called up. The Alex Senior School in London was better because there I was doing algebra but when I got to Wickford School they were not. I took my eleven-plus in Watford and I failed. If you passed, you went to a technical or grammar school.

Mr Reeves

Art or building

In 1941 we came down here from Ilford. We originally lodged with Tom Rushbrook who worked on the farm and lived in a red-brick cottage at the bottom of Kembles Hill. I went to Rettendon School with his son Alan for a few months before going to Wickford Junior School. There, our headteacher was Mr Kitson who gave me the cane a few times; I cannot remember why but he did not need a reason. Then I went to Wickford Senior School where Miss Amos was my teacher and from there to Chelmsford Technical School where you could take art, engineering, commerce or building. I took building and took an apprenticeship in plumbing when I left.

Alan Goddard

Teachers from Wickford Senior School, 1950. From left to right, back row: Mr Brooks, Mr Pelmear, Mr Ross, Mr Rackham, Mr Lovelack, Mr Gash, Mr Ryman, Mr Phillips, Mr Richards, Mr Fountain, Mr Crock, Miss Warren. Front row: Miss Fullerton, Miss Hope, Miss Franklin, Stella Medcalf, Mr Rowes, Mrs Roebuck, Miss Riggs, Mrs Rose, Mary Cockie.

three
Wickford Market

Wickford cattle market at the beginning of the 1900s.

Wickford market in the 1930s.

Cows in the High Street

Wickford market was nothing like it is now. On market day, I hated going to school because the cows, bulls and sheep were driven through the High Street. One man would stand in front and one man behind waving their hands and if the cows came to an open gateway they had a great ambition to go through it. I used to get in somebody's garden and shut the gate until they had gone. Pigs were transported in a cart with a net over them. Where the Castle Hotel was, they had sheep pens and would tie up the bulls and cows. The auctioneer would stand up on big flat boards and then shout out gibberish and the farmers would bid. The next day, on our way to cookery classes, we used to slide down the big ramp that they used for sheep to walk up to get into the vehicles. I was always late for cookery.

Queenie Thorington

A cup of tea

The market was open on a Monday and the cattle used to walk up the High Street. The rabbits and the poultry were sold where the Castle used to be. The cattle market was where Boots the chemist is now. They auctioned them like they do on the telly. Behind Hall's, there was a tin hut with wooden seats. That's where the farmers got a cup of tea. My mum worked there and they had a spoon on a piece of elastic which you pulled down to stir your tea and it would spring back.

Emily Babbage

A fishmonger selling from his stall on a Monday morning.

Smelly but interesting

In the '60s, I thought Wickford was lovely. It was a large sleepy village which only came to life on market day. I used to buy my fish and meat out the back of a van. There was one character who wore a fez and shouted out and sold linen and towels. There were a couple of really nice china stalls, a costume jewellery stall, they sold everything. They also had a livestock market that they had on the corner of Market Road which again was very interesting, smelly ,but interesting. They had sheep and chickens.

Doreen Reed

Beautiful sausages

My grandfather Franklin had a butcher's shop at the Broadway end of the High Street and used to go to the market to buy cattle and sheep for his slaughterhouse. His two sons were also butchers. Grandma prepared and cooked the brawn. On a Friday night I helped to make 5cwt of sausages. The meat was rammed into the machine and then I turned

Shopping at the market.

the handle to squash it out into the skin on the end of a brass tube. I used to knot them, eight to a pound, and then I hung them on stringers and put them in the refrigerator. They were beautiful sausages but when my grandfather died the recipe died with him.

Peter Hall

Truant from school

There was an unmade path going right up the side of the railway which led to the market. When I was about seven, I used to play truant from school and go down to the market. Although my brother had a green-grocer's shop, at Christmas I used to sell holly wreaths for him on the market. In the fifties, my mum used to buy chickens from the market and keep them in our orchard at Bruce Grove.

Fred Smith

What will you give me for this?

It was a real market where they used to bring their lorries to the front. There were all these little shacks that had bits and pieces in. The meat was sold from the back of a lorry and the butcher would say, 'What will you give me for this?' and he would then clap his hands. There was Alf Cohen, who also sold from the back of his lorry. He sold everything. He used to throw them in the air and say, 'What will you give me for this ?' and then he would name his price and gradually come down. The market was so cheap that we would buy most of our Christmas presents there. Further down the market, they used to put big sheets on the ground where they laid out their goods. There was a little café behind Woolworths where all the market people went. In the middle of the market, there was a big hall where they held functions such as weddings and parties.

Doreen Williams

Hall's horticultural shop in the High Street.

A market stall selling fabric in the 1960s.

Time to settle up

Monday was a very busy day in Wickford and the farmers used to come and pay their accounts. One farmer I remember was Joe Livermore; he was a jovial cockney type, always cheerful. The Keelings were smashing people. We used to do quite a bit of business with Jack and Joe Keeling. They hired out the threshing machines which were driven by steam engines and would thresh the corn in the field. They would bundle it up and bring it to the machine by horse and cart or tractor and the men would throw it into the machine. In those days, they had these great big 2¼cwt sacks of wheat which we had to put on the lorries by a pulley and bring them back to the store. During carnival time, we would dress the horses and carts up and enter them. The horses were gradually phased out for lorries.

Roy Hall

Mostly ex-servicemen

After the war, my family moved to Wickford. When my brother was demobbed, we started up a horticultural business. It was hard work but the outlay was small. We grew tomatoes, peas, beans and cabbages which we sold at Wickford market. It used to be buzzing with at least sixty smallholders, mostly ex-servicemen. Over time we gradually went over to raising chickens and pigs. We used to buy our agricultural items from Darby's and they did our repairs.

Norman Simmons

A stroll through the market.

four

Wickford at Work

Work at fourteen

Before the First World War, my father was a carpenter and joiner and built houses by hand – the staircases, windows and roofs, which took a long time. Nowadays these things are built off-site and brought by lorry. I expect they can build 100 houses now in the same time it took to build one. I started work in a sweet shop and teashop in Brentwood High Street as a waitress for seven shillings a week. The tips went into a central pool where they were supposed to share out equally but I think they used to cheat as I never got much. I did not like working weekends and bank holidays as my family did things then, so I left. I stayed at home for a time and then I got a job in a new Woolworths in Hamlet Court Road, Westcliff and each day I caught the steam train down to Southend and then a tram to Hamlet Court Road. I was there for about three years. In my mother's day, the barges would come right up the River Crouch to Battlesbridge and stop there. The captains would take on the fourteen-year-old boys and that was the end of their schooldays and they would stay away for years.

Queenie Thorington

Shotgate Farm

Uncle Tom and Dad and one of my aunts did most of the work on the farm. We had chickens, rabbits, geese, cows and pigs who ran around at the top of the yard. The pigs would be taken away, killed and then brought back so we could cure the bacon by hanging it in the great big chimney. Gran made our own sausages and cooked on an old range which she kept alight all the time. They chopped the meat up on a table which they used for everything else but it did nobody any harm. At harvest time everybody used to muck in. They started at seven and worked through till dark. Mother and I used to take a big basket out to the workers, full of food. I would ride on the carts and all the family came and helped, including Jackie, my niece. We hired the threshing machine from Keelings. All the corn would go to Battlesbridge to the mill. All our farm machinery went into Darby's for repair. First thing in the morning, we milked the eighteen cows by hand. When milk parlours came in, we gave up the cows because it cost too much money to convert. We put the work out to Howard's, the milk people.

Joan Cox

Darby's

In 1952, when I was fifteen, I started working for Darby's as a mate and earned ninepence

Joan Cox helping with the harvest, 1924.

farthing an hour, that's old money. The firm started in 1862 when it came to Runwell Road, Wickford to a works called Stileman's. The firm was on both sides of the road and extended from the Ford garage to the cricket field entrance. It did anything to do with farming. It was in the days when farming was going from candles to electric light. Darby's had a number of different sections. There was a carpenter's shop, which repaired wagons and anything connected with wood. The wheelwrights made the wagon wheels. The foreman of the tractor shop was Harold Lodge. Bill Brockersly and Percy White were his two mechanics. They repaired tractors and so on. Bill Brooks was the lathe turner and

fitter; he later became one of two welders. Ben Playle was the electrician and I repaired and maintained stationary engines. That was any engine bolted down and driven by the driving belts of generators. In the garage there were as many as fourteen vans and Don Sainsbury and Jim Flanigan were the drivers of the firm's two lorries. Jack Franklin was the foreman who, during the war, was the Chief Fire Officer of Wickford. The mechanics maintained the firm's vehicles and also most of the farmers' transport. The farmers would come in on Monday, market day, with their problems. In the early days, mechanics would go out on motorbikes to carry out the repairs to generators and threshing machines

Roy Simpson's father working at Darby's.

but later they went out in vans. Bill Leper played the important role of storeman. In those days, there were about thirty working for the firm plus the boys who were training. Sidney Darby was the real character but he was before my time. I heard he used to smoke a pipe and apparently if he wanted to cross the road he would hold his hand up and stop the traffic; not that there was much traffic around in those days! I believe he died in 1951. Jack Stock was a managing director and another character. Mr Churcher was another director. Connie Ford was a Darby. Miss Knight ran the office; she was also a shareholder. When farms started going over from hand milking to milking parlours, we installed and maintained them. They were either engine- or electric-driven. I got around all the farms and it was a good place to learn. The old Darby Digger, for which the firm is famous, was pulled behind a steam engine. They exported them out to Egypt. They were a bit too heavy for the soil round here. The firm also made the Darby All Weather Wheel, which was an iron wheel with angle iron bolted on the wheels so that it would not sink down into the mud. In 1966 they had a fire which started in the old thatched cottage, which was once the old farmhouse. I worked there until 1978, when I started to work for myself repairing lawn-mowers and so on.

Stan Gregory

Harvest time

The horses did the ploughing and during harvest we would sit under the haystacks to shade us from the sun and we would watch the threshing machines. We longed to help but they would not let us. Wickford was wonder-ful in those days. Nell Cooling would stand at her tiny stall in front of her house in the London Road and sell jams and honey. Percy the cowman and his brother would come in to milk the cows by hand. There were no machines in those days. They poured the milk into little churns and we took it to the customers, one of whom was Woods Garage along the London Road. One lady used to give us plums. My grandmother made our butter, by hand, in the dairy. The Porters lived in the bungalow next door to my grandfather.

Doris Orton

Carter and Ward

Carter and Ward started off doing war damage. They had an open-back truck and used to put up the plasterboard and mend windows after a raid.

Yvonne Wilkinson

Fire service

Grandfather was a boy entrant in the private Billericay fire brigade and became one of the mainstays in Wickford. He told me that the fire service in Wickford consisted of a hand-cart, several ladders, a basic pump, a bucket and a lot of pulling power. I think it was safe to say that when he got to the fire it was almost out.

Trevor Williams

All I wanted to do was leave school

I left school when I was fourteen, that's all we wanted to do, but once I started work I wished I was back again. My first job was at Darby's. Jack Stock was the foreman. I knew old Sidney C. Darby, the owner, he was a right eccentric. He had cobwebs hanging from his hat. In the morning he would come out and shout across to Jack Stock who lived opposite, 'Hello Stock, what you doing today only I want that boy to come and cut my grass.' I had to go and do it. I got eighteen and six a week. It was a lot of money in those days. I

Mr Archer of Shotgate Farm ploughing with a team of horses, 1928.

was not at Darby's for very long. I did not like being closed in. After working for Darby's, I went to Keelings in Crays Hill for six years on a threshing machine. I used to put the corn into the drum and carry the sacks away. It was hard work. My father was the foreman of Chichester Farm and he asked if I wanted to be the tractor driver and so at twenty-four I became a tractor driver.

Ernie Woods

Locked gates

During the fifties, when I was thirty, I worked in Runwell Hospital's nursing home where the patients used to try and cadge fags off us. Each night a man used to lock the gates. They don't now, of course.

Emily Babbage

Quality not quantity

As a child, during the war, I belonged to the Mala School of Dancing and at Christmas we performed a pantomime for the soldiers who were convalescing at Runwell Hospital. When I was sixteen, in the fifties, I worked for Schofield and Martin's shop and the post office but I really wanted to be a nurse. I stayed for six months then took up children's nursing at Hutton Residential School. My mum worked at Runwell Hospital and was asked if I would like to work there. I got the post but did not want to start at the bottom again. To my surprise, they agreed for me to start as a second-year student. We had different-coloured uniforms with a blue stripe for each year we had completed. The pay was not much and cleaning was part of the regime. We changed wards every three months. One

Ward Sister was very strict and always said she wanted 'Quality not quantity' but she was an excellent tutor and gave her students a solid grounding. Unfortunately, she is dead now but the ward she managed was renamed the Clara Hold Ward in her honour. The patients were really looked after. My brother worked on the hospital farm as a cowhand for many years. I was there from 1956 and left as a Ward Sister in 1967. I left to have my son then became a Community Nurse for eleven years.

Yvonne Wilkinson

I did not understand

My uncle, Arthur Bridge, drove lorries for Matthews and used to go up to Runwell Hospital to collect the wheat from the farm. As a kid, I did not understand and I would sit in the cab with all these strange people going by and I would be terrified. My uncle and Stan Percival would take me up to London to the British Oil and Cake Mills in Silvertown and we would sing at the top of our voices all the way there and back.

Mr Barker

Heating engineer

I was born in Fulham and came down to Wickford in 1957 because the houses were cheaper. I was a self-employed plumber and heating engineer. Wickford was a lot smaller then and has gradually built up over the years.

A Matthews lorry loaded with wheat, 1930s. From left to right: B. Holt, George Bridge, Edward Bridge, Stan Percival, T. Frost.

There was even a brickworks in Nevendon Road.

Eddie Noyes

Redundancy

I worked as a boilerman in Bell Cleaners opposite the old post office in Southend Road. We used steam irons and presses. I worked there for ten years and then they sold out and I was out of a job.

Mr Spindler

Thirty bob a week

I worked on Bakers Farm with the farmer's family. I was there for a long while and got paid thirty bob a week. I used to do haymaking, drive a horse and work on the threshing machines, throwing the corn into the machines and extracting the corn. The smell and atmosphere of the farm was beautiful but today it is all chemicals.

Fred Smith

Hall's horticultural shop.

Hall's

Hall's corn and seed merchants started in 1903 in Timberlog Lane in Basildon. Grandfather bought the Old Croft House which was behind Adrian's. He went to a sale and bought three acres of land which led down to the river. There were three sons: Peter, Sidney and John, John being my father. He built the Old Croft and the New Croft House, which is now the Duke. Then he built three more terraced houses and my mother and father lived in the end one, Bridge End, where I was born. Twenty-four years later I got married and went back to live in the same house. Things started to develop and we had about five or six acres. We would make hay during the summer months. Gradually my uncles dissolved the partnership and my father took over and he brought me and my brother in, while Peter went into engineering. We formed a limited company and went from strength to strength and served most of the farmers in the district. My father bought me a lorry and I did the London trip for twenty-two years, driving up to Victoria Docks early in the morning with corn and bringing back animal feeds. There was no traffic on the road in those days, especially at that time in the morning. It has all changed now; the docks have gone. As Basildon Development Corporation compulsorily purchased the farms in the eighties, business started to fall off and so we diversified and went into gardening.

Roy Hall

Workers at the brickfields in Nevendon Road in the 1930s.

Grandad's farm

My grandad had Jackson and Hunt's farm out at Ramsden Heath and I used to help him with the cattle and so on. When the bluebells were out, we would pick them and sell them in the market. There was a shop up the road that had all these empty bottles round the back and we would pick them up and take them round the front of the shop and get money on them.

Barrie Adcock

Chairmaker

I met my husband playing tennis at Battlesbridge, a village close by, and got married in 1940. He had his own business as a chairmaker in Shoreditch, London, an area which is famous for furniture.

Joan Cox

Gravedigger

I started gravedigging in 1962 when Mr Carter the undertaker came up to our flower shop, Eileen's, one day and asked if I could dig a grave for him in Wickford churchyard as he was stuck for a gravedigger and that is how I started. The oldest person I dug a grave for was 200 years old. She was dug up while they were building some new houses in Great Wakering. It's hard work but when you're young you don't take any notice of it. I've been out at half past four in the morning in the summer, directly the sun comes up.

Ernie Woods

I worked in London

I was fourteen when I left school and I started work at Pardy and Johnson in Wickford. I then went to the Co-op, in the butchery office. I

Joan Cox's father, Mr Archer, in 1960 on his tractor at Shotgate Farm.

was there till 1940, when I left. Dad said to me, 'You had better find yourself a job or they will call you up.' A girl who lived over the road worked at Cooks of St Paul's and suggested I applied there. I was successful and worked for them for a couple of years. I would cycle up to Wickford station and leave the bike unchained there all day. Nobody stole it! I would then travel up to London by train. I would leave work at 4 p.m. and we would run to St Paul's station and catch the 4.18 and be in Wickford by five and then I would cycle home. They were the old steam trains then and were never late.

Joan Cox

Twelve and six a dozen

Mum worked at home during the war and made blouses for twelve and six a dozen. She used a treadle machine and when we got home from school we used to help by doing the shoulder pads just like sausages while mum got our tea.

Yvonne Wilkinson

Their first office junior

I left school at fourteen but did not travel far, just across the road to Hallmark Hatchery where I was their first office junior. I did the filing, answered the phone and made the tea, all for fifteen shillings a week, old money. There were about five in the office. The firm sold day-old chicks and advertised them in the *News Of The World* and charged twenty-five shillings for the best ones but they were good layers. I stayed there until I married and then when my daughter went to school I went in at lunchtimes. When she got older, I went back

Yvonne Wilkinson, aged nineteen, outside her bungalow.

part-time and when his secretary left I worked for the boss.

Shirley Dine

Luncheon vouchers

I worked in London and would run if I heard the train coming, all the way down to the station from Highcliff Road and then climb over the bridge. I would get on the steam train out of breath. It took only an hour to get up to London and I had to make sure I caught it because if I missed it I had to wait an hour for the next one. We never got home from work until seven or half past. We would do much longer hours. I earned about four pounds a week in those days. We used to get luncheon vouchers but if you did not use them some of the shops would take them for all sorts of things. I used to meet a girl friend for lunch and we would always go into Lyons Corner House and have sausage and chips and a piece of apple tart. The waitresses wore black dresses and white aprons.

Mrs Livermore

We made all types of wreaths

I was digging a grave at Rettendon one day and I asked Eileen, my wife, if she would like to come with me. While I was digging, Eileen went over and looked at a grave which had some old wreaths on it. We took these home and made them up. That was the beginning of Eileen's the florists. She went to London and got her City and Guilds. We made all types of wreaths – dogs, anything. The most unusual wreath we made was a bullock for a slaughterman who had died. It stood about 4ft high and was as long as a settee. It stood in the corner at Upminster crematorium and people thought it was real. She made it out of moss and wire. She was the first one to put ribbon round these modern wreaths. In the old days we used to put all greenery round them.

Ernie Woods (on behalf of Eileen)

Wickford was a village

When I was a teenager and going up to London, everybody knew each other on the train. Wickford was a village.

Val Dowman

Last in, first out

After the war, I came out of farming and went to work for Shell for three months. I was offered a good job but there were redundancies and it was last in, first out and so I found myself searching for a job. So I went to work for Clark Chapmans in Basildon. All stainless steel, it was hard work and I was there for about thirty years.

Mr Williams

Policing

We had only one policeman, Sergeant Brewer. He was a great big man and so had to have a great big bike and we were all frightened of him. Not like now. He stood on the corner and would say, 'You! What are you doing?'

Emily Babbage

Petticoat government

In September 1941 I obtained a post at Wickford Senior School, which is now the junior school, in Market Road. My pupils' ages ranged from eleven upwards and there were only 350 of them. They came in busloads from all the surrounding areas, including the Hanningfields and Woodham Ferrers, which shows how the area has grown over the years. By 1984 we had reached 1,500 pupils at Beauchamps. The figures have gone down now to about 1,000 or 1,100. When I joined the school, there were only two men on the staff because the rest were in the forces. There was the head and one other and so it was petticoat government but we did a darned good job. Regularly I meet with the girls and one or two of the boys who came with me in 1942 at the age of eleven. They are now seventy-four and we meet about every three or four months at each other's houses. One of the

Constable House pupils at Beauchamps School's sports day in the 1960s.

teachers who normally comes is Mrs Mason. My first headmaster was Mr Rose, who was a very gifted man, very artistic. Mr Ward and Mr Davis were others.

The kids in those days did not take advantage. You started off being pretty strict then, when you had them, you could relax. There were all sorts of tricks we had to keep control. A lot of them would not be allowed now. One of the things we used to do with the headmaster's permission was to frisk the pockets of the kids' jackets, which hung on pegs outside the classroom, for cigarettes. One day I found a set of false teeth. I went back into the classroom and said, 'You know what I've been doing but somebody had something very strange in their pocket, perhaps they would like to come and talk to me after lessons.' A boy came out and hung his head and said, 'Is it a set of teeth?' I nodded and he hung his head before going on, 'They're my mum's. We had a row and I saw them on the bathroom windowsill and so I took them!' Over a period of forty years I must have had most of the children from Wickford through my hands. Not only them but their parents and grandparents.

I had a friend, who was a teacher at the school and was only 5ft 2in. She was always getting teased. One day, two of the men picked her up and put her on the cupboards in the corridor. She struggled to get down. I don't know what the children thought as they passed. So there was a class without a teacher and the deputy head took her class. When she got down, the deputy head said, 'Where were you? I had to take your class.' Sheepishly she replied, 'They put me up on a cupboard and I could not get down.' The deputy head said, 'What a load of rubbish.' In the end, I had to confirm her story.

Mary Cockie (Miss Amos)

You still smoking?

When I first started smoking, I didn't want to get caught and so I used to take a drag and then turn the cigarette inside my cupped hand. One day I was walking down the road with my mates and a Wickford copper, whom my

From left to right: Jean Hall, Margaret Wilson, Geoffrey Pearl, Alan Goddard.

father knew well, came up and said 'Hello, young Williams.' He caught hold of my hand with the cigarette in and crushed it. I went home with third degree burns and I thought, 'What do I tell my mum?', not realising that she could smell the smoke on my breath. I told her I'd climbed over some barbed wire fence and my hand had slipped. Three or four months later, at the Air Training Corps, the policeman confronted me and asked 'You still smoking?'

Trevor Williams

Star, News and Standard

Years ago, the most popular paper was the *Daily Mirror* and that was because of 'Jane', the adult comic strip, particularly with the soldiers during the war. We used to sell the *Evening News*, *Standard* and the *Evening Star*. The most chaotic night was Saturday night. Very few people had television and they all gathered in the shop for the football results. My father supported

Ipswich; Gordon Carter, the undertaker, supported the Southern United team; Ron Mayes used to play for Chelsea; Mr Holten came from Norfolk and so he supported Norwich. Not only that, the police used to walk in and so if you wanted a policeman or if somebody died on a Saturday night, you were out of luck unless you looked in the shop. The papers came down on the train and although I was very young, Dad and I used to pick them up at about 4.15 in the morning. You could set your watch by the trains. The guards would help us take the papers off. We did wholesale as well as retail. We used to do the whole of the district, out as far as Howe Green and Basildon. In fact we supplied all of the Martin's shops.

Barrie Adcock

Cutthroat razors

I left school at fourteen and started with Mr Henry, the barber, in the Broadway opposite

The Annual Dinner of the Wickford Chamber of Trade and Industry. Mr Adcock Snr. is third from the right at the front. Barrie Adcock is last on the left by the door.

the Swan. My hand was shaking the first time I shaved someone with a cutthroat razor. One day, my dad was having his hair cut and Mr Henry said that his son had just been called up and he wanted somebody he could train. My dad piped up, 'My lad is leaving school and needs a job.' and that was it. My dad thought it was better than me becoming an errand boy because he did not think I was strong enough to push the pedals on their bikes. At first I had to sweep up, then he let me lather the customers for their shave with the cutthroat razor while the boss cut their hair. There were more shaves done in those days. When he'd finished, I put any cream on and then brushed them down. That first day I was very tired and my feet were sore. Normally you had to pay to learn the trade but Mr Henry waived that and paid me five shillings a week plus any tips. It was not as well paid as some other jobs but I was learning a trade. We worked from eight o'clock in the morning until seven at night. We charged sixpence for a haircut for men, threepence for a shave and fourpence for a boy's haircut. With the kids, we used to put a plank across the chair. When I started, there was Mr Henry, another fellow called Eric Bird and myself. The gents was downstairs and the ladies was up. My only regret was that I did not learn ladies' hairdressing. I started with a pair of electric clippers but you still had to have a pair of hand clippers because some customers liked them. Mr Henry was going to hand the shop over to his son but he got killed during the war. Hairstyles have changed over the years. I remember the Boston. Then there was the DA, something to do with a certain part of a duck's anatomy. There was the Tony Curtis; the sides were swept back. Unfortunately, I did not do styling. I was a short back and sides man.

Mr Reeves

You had to rely on tips

I left school at fourteen and went to work at Madam Dore's, doing hairdressing. I did a five years' apprenticeship, three years' learning and two years as an improver. I received ten shillings a week for the first three years and that went up to twelve and six the last two years. You had to rely on tips. When I had the children, I gave up going out to work but did some hairdressing at home. It did not work out and so I went up to the Metal Box Company doing chequebooks.

Doreen Williams

Sergeant Brewer

I played football at school and cricket in the street. We used to pinch people's palings off their fences for a cricket bat. Today it would have been criminal. Sergeant Brewer, he was a spoilsport. He would come up and take the rubber off our catapults but we would go to the saddler's shop, where the Midland Bank used to be, and get another piece of elastic and make another one. We put bottles and cans on the wall and knocked them down.

Fred Smith

Now the boot is on the other foot

I don't go down to the shops any more because of my health but I have such good neighbours around me that I don't have to. I have carers and I taught most of them. When they first come and I open the door, they step back in surprise and say, 'It's Miss Amos!' I was caring for them at school and now the boot is on the other foot. I taught the one that comes here at the moment, Linda. They were all nice girls. Some of the girls had brothers who were interested in old motorbikes and my husband's hobby was restoring classic cars of the 1940s and sometimes we would meet these boys at the car rallies. When I meet some of my ex-pupils in town, they give me a lovely hug. I was rather touched one day when a youngster ran up to me and shouted out to her grandad, 'That's my mummy's teacher.'

Mary Cockie (Miss Amos)

Estate agents

Before the war until 1959, we were in Hovefields House. We assisted folk to build, buy and manage homes. One of our clients whose houses we managed was Frederick Arthur Mills of the now preserved The Haven, Third Avenue, Dunton Hills Estate. In the thirties, we also managed for Raymond Walter Bloust of the houseboat Fen Haven, Woodham Ferrers. After the war, there was a labour shortage and Basildon was designated as a New Town and required surveyors to negotiate the compulsory purchase of land. I used to get recommended from client to client. In order not to miss out on business opportunities, I worked long hours including evenings. In 1959 we moved offices to a newly built one in Pitsea which we leased from Roger Howard. We were there for twenty-eight years then Roger Howard died and the agents wanted to change the lease and so we looked elsewhere and found premises in Wickford in 1987.

Reg Iles

The Apprenticeship Master scheme

I became an apprentice bricklayer with Carter and Ward in 1947, in company with Alan Goddard and forty other boys. We built five pairs of houses near St Catherine's church, under the Apprenticeship Master scheme. I fixed the commemorative plaque on the wall of one of the houses in Highcliff Road. Jackie Joyce was one of the very first people to move into one in September 1947. I laid my very

Apprentices who built the houses in Highcliff Road under the Apprentice scheme in 1949. Note the plaque on the wall.

first brick in that house of hers. I built a little brick screen wall in the outhouse, it was 3ft high and four bricks long and I took a lot of trouble. I had just finished it when Bill Young, the supervisor, came up and said 'That's a load of rubbish!' and he put his boot through it.

John Dowman and Jackie Joyce

Plumbing apprentice

I came out of college and started as a plumbing apprentice and for a few months worked on the Apprenticeship Master scheme with John Dowman on the Highcliff site and then I went to Runwell Hospital as a maintenance apprentice. I did not learn much because all I did was unblock sinks and fit tap washers but it was great for sport. When I was twenty-one, I got called up to do my National Service in the Royal Air Force. The pay was not good and I was well over twenty before I earned ten pounds. When I was demobbed I obtained a job as a plumber with Roy Thompson for a while before moving to the laboratory at the Mobil Oil Company for the next thirty-four years, until I retired.

Alan Goddard

Mr and Mrs Simmons today.

We fight to get as much as we can

I have been a member of Runwell Parish Council for twelve years and nine of those as chairman. I got involved when a customer came into the shop and I happened to say that I would like to give something back to society. Roy Dockerill had been on the council for a number of years and he proposed me. The biggest issue is trying to get decent facilities for Wickford and Runwell. Basildon and Chelmsford always take the lion's share and we fight to get as much as we can. Runwell Hospital is a brownfield site and they are going to build on it. There are 230 acres altogether. There used to be a wonderful hall there, which is just going to be bulldozed down but they are leaving the church. It was proposed originally to build 340 houses, then it went up to over 500 and now it is 600. Now 20 per cent of the houses have to be affordable houses.

Norman Simmons

Care worker

The council wanted someone for the Children's Department in Neverdon Road for six weeks. I went and stayed for six years. The department then transferred to Social Services and we moved to Corringham. Then we moved to Billericay and I finished up as a Community Officer and retired in 1982. I was working for the Voluntary Warden Scheme and had the job of organising it. We started a Helping Hands scheme because we needed more back-up.

Shirley Dines

He was just mad on his work

My father had the corn merchants, Hall's, but I did not want to do that and so I went into an engineering firm called Edward Farr, as an apprentice welder. I got qualified at night school. The firm no longer exists. When I started, they were still doing war work. I was in the main workshop for about two years and then I got called up for my National Service and on returning I carried on as a welder for the next forty years. My father worked hard, seven days a week, and only ever had one week's holiday, as far as I can remember. He was just mad on his work. My two brothers worked for him. He had a great crushing machine which ground the corn from the local farms for animal food. Sometimes they worked all night. On occasions, I gave them a hand but it was hard work, especially if the oats were wet.

Peter Hall

Odd-job man

I was only a boy when I started my first job with Harris Cakes in Nevendon Road. I remember going to Colchester with him and being so cold I started to cry and the smell of the cakes made me feel sick. I soon left there and went to work for a firm in Lower Southend Road called Simpson's Shop on Wheels; he delivered soap powders, paraffin, anything. After that, I did all sorts of jobs like window cleaning, anything. My brother Ron came out of the Army after serving in the 8th Army in Egypt and set up a greengrocer's shop which he rented off Hall's. It is now a fast-food shop.

Fred Smith

A daily domestic

I started out doing a Saturday job until I left school at fourteen, then I went as a daily domestic at Millhurst but unfortunately I

Smith's greengrocery shop, 1950.

Roy Simpson's father, who worked for English the Butcher's in the mid-1930s.

slipped down the stairs, broke my ankle and so I could not work. There was no sickness leave in those days and so I had to pack it in. When my leg got better, I got a job at a place called Firs Hall, Beggars Hill. My elder brother had worked there as chauffeur and then he became a general assistant helping in the stable and my sister worked there as an in-between maid. My godmother let me know about the job that was going at Mrs Bradbridge's so I took it. There was a cook , a parlourmaid and myself. One night, the lady came to me and said, 'Violet, I'm afraid I'm going to have to let you go because I'm afraid I have to cut back and as you were the last person I employed it's got to be you.' I had a month's notice. I was not really bothered because there were a lot of big houses at Ingatestone and Mill Green. I was not out of work long and at the end of the month I got a job with the Sewells, who did a lot with Charrington's beers. The lady was so nice and asked me to sit with the family for my meals but I told her it would not be practical as I could not do the washing-up between serving at the table. During the war I worked at Marconi's in Chelmsford.

Mrs Reeves

Christ Church

In 1971, due to the proposed ring road and declining membership, the Methodist and Congregational churches amalgamated, becoming Christ Church. They were in the High Street opposite Market Road. We could not do any alterations because they were going to bring the ring road right through it. It went to the House of Lords but it took so long that we obtained a bit of land next to Somerfields.

Beryl Humphrey

five
Flooding

Canoeing up the High Street 1958.

The water swirled round us

In 1958, when I was about eleven, I woke up one morning to torrential rain and the river Crouch flowing down Sugden Avenue, cutting us off. My friend and I went into Wickford and saw rowing boats at each end of the High Street and an Army DUKW amphibious vehicle coming up the road. We got in a rowing boat while the water swirled round us. Suddenly I lost an oar and we went round and round. Luckily the other boat caught us and pulled us into the shallow water. It was good fun.

Joyce Ward

1953 floods

I was at my uncle's house playing cards in 1953 when the storm broke. Luckily somebody had lent me a Land Rover and so we struggled home to the London Road. When I got up the next morning, Wickford was under water. Mr Carter, the undertaker, telephoned me and said that he knew I had the Land Rover and could I nip down to Mr Adcock the newsagent as everything was under water. When I got to the shop in the High Street, everything was floating around but luckily the fuses had blown so there was no danger of getting electrocuted.

Ernie Woods

Canvey refugees

During the 1953 floods, we had to close the school and had all the refugees from Canvey sleeping along the top corridor. Usually, during the normal floods, there would be two or three inches of water in the main hall.

Mrs Cockie (Miss Amos)

Above: The flooded High Street, looking down on the Castle public house.

Right: A milkman delivering milk during the floods.

We took it in our stride

We moved to Shotgate just before the war and every year Wickford got flooded but we took it in our stride. Carter and Ward, the builders, used to put planks down and we would cross the road on these or they would ferry people across in a flat-bottomed boat. In 1958 it started off as a drizzle and it got heavier and heavier and there was thunder and lightning, it absolutely teemed down. Within hours, the park was a huge lake. All the roads became rivers. John, my fiancé, propped his motorbike outside my mother's and it got swept away. We were stranded. To get into the town centre, we went as far as we could then went up the railway embankment and walked along.

Yvonne Wilkinson

Southend lights

It was a lovely day in September 1958 so I took my three children to see the lights at Southend and left my husband at home. As we got on the

Carter and Ward's DUKW beating the floods.

homeward bound bus it started to rain. We had to get off the bus at the Quart Pot because the roads were flooded. A man came along with a tractor and took us round to Church End Road. We were lucky that our bungalow was high up.

Emily Babbage

home because right under the bridge into Wickford was a milk float and a car stuck in the middle of the water. I ended up going round Battlesbridge. I understand that some bloke sailed his boat along the floods.

Eddie Noyes

Miss Powderpuff

In 1968 my daughter was six and was Miss Powderpuff in the carnival. It poured with rain and flooded that day. I could not get us

Petition

Following the river floods, Joyce came round with a petition. That's how we met. We formed a Community Association. A

Joyce's flooded bungalow, 1958.

councillor came round and we learned from him that the council was thinking of compulsorily purchasing our estate. Tom Fowler down the road called a meeting which was held in my house. We included three issues on the agenda: flooding, no running water (we had a standpipe) and compulsory purchase.

Ken Ward

Community Association

At first we were just a group of residents with a grievance then we decided to set up a committee. Two years later they started to put the water in and my dad dug a trench down our garden to connect it up. He said he was not going to pay their prices for labouring. We set up a collection fund for the unmade road and asked people to

pay sixpence a week each towards the hardcore. Some people who did not have a car would not pay; some paid more. We never heard from the council but we learned they were going to build on Barn Hall instead.

Joyce Ward

A floating coffin

In 1958 it started to rain and rain; there were torrents! Somebody telephoned my father and said that he had better get down to our shop, Adcock's the newsagents. So my father, Derek Richardson, Brian Richardson, Alma Richardson and I went to the shop. I have never seen a river come up so fast. That day we had just had our refrigerator filled with ice cream. I turned off the electric and tried to shift it but

A lorry making waves outside Adcock's newsagents.

the water was pouring into the shop. Within half an hour the water was up to my waist. A petrol tanker sped past, causing a tidal wave which burst open the double doors and threw me back, hitting my head against the counter. We staggered upstairs with whatever we could rescue and were marooned up there for three days. I was watching things float past when, I could not believe my eyes, there was this empty coffin drifting past. Later I found out that somebody had opened the gates at the back of Carter's the funeral directors and the coffin had started out on its journey. After a while I tried to get out the back but, as I did so, the current caught me and swept me along. I tried to stop myself and finally managed to catch hold of a 'Keep Left' sign. I held on, catching my breath, then I struggled back against the surging current. After three days, Carter's came along with their DWYK lorry and rescued us. It took us some time to recover financially.

Barrie Adcock

A walk on the railway

I had to go on the train to Rayleigh to get the shopping because the shops were all flooded. It did not flood every year, only on two or three occasions. The two bad years were 1940 something and 1953. A few friends had been to the Swan and the Castle and could not get home and so we offered them a cup of tea and a sandwich and told them they could sleep on the floor if they liked but they refused, saying, 'No, we'll paddle home.' They walked along the railway line and got off at the Wick Lane level crossing to get to Mount Road. The water was so deep that it half-filled a double-decker bus. Carter and Ward had a DWYK out, a lorry that went on land or floated. It went up and down the High Street ferrying people about. The mess was terrible and when the water went down everywhere was covered in a film of mud. The Castle and

the Swan's beer cellars were flooded right up to the top.

Doreen Williams

It was down to my knees

They always finish the carnival in a field and we had just got there when it started raining. I had a short woollen dress on but by the time I got home it was down to my knees.

Yvonne Abbott

Floating turkeys

Our church feeds the carnival and one year the weather was fine until about 2.30 p.m. when suddenly it poured down. Mr and Mrs Hodges put everything in the car and headed for home but we found we could not get

The High Street in the winter of 1947.

under the bridge and so we decided to go up Castledon Road. That was fatal. We went straight into the water and there we stuck. We sat there a while and then went into a farm for help and saw all these dead turkeys floating about from the freezer.

Beryl Humphrey

We would walk across the fields

In 1947 I remember the winter and the snow. My gran lived in the Old School House and we would walk across the fields to see her. The snow was right up to our calves. 1963 was just as bad.

Mrs Livermore

Winter of 1947

My dad worked for the council on road maintenance. I remember the snow in 1947. You could not get out the door. All the roads were blocked. He could not get out to work and so he went to clear the snow.

Mr Barker

Three feet of snow

We moved to Wickford in 1947 in three feet of snow. It was a couple of feet deep in the unmade roads. Many of the houses and shops were just wooden shacks then and over the years I have seen many changes in the town.

William Mead

six

Wickford at Play

Salvation Army films

There was a cinema in the Salvation Army huts in Jersey Gardens. It used to cost sixpence to get in. When it rained it would pitter patter on the corrugated roof and you could not hear the film. Often the film broke down and everybody whistled. One picture I remember was *Mandy*, about a little deaf and dumb girl. Next door was a little wool shop which had in it all the clothes that were in the film. My mum would send us to Saturday morning pictures and we would see Roy Rogers, Laurel and Hardy, Abbott and Costello and Charlie Chaplin. They also held Remembrance Day at the cinema and everybody would stand to attention while they played the Last Post. When we were too young for a film, we would wait outside and ask an adult to take us in but there were some people who were not very nice! My mum and gran often went to the pictures.

Mrs Livermore

Carlton cinema

There was the Carlton cinema which was later converted to Woolworths. I remember after the war, when I was eleven, the school took us to see a newsreel of Belsen. It was horrible, all those dead bodies. Most of the kids were upset. Sometimes we would go to Saturday morning children's pictures and see cartoons and Charlie Chaplin. The tickets were threepence.

Yvonne Wilkinson

Some of the businesspeople of Wickford turning on the High Street Christmas lights from the Carlton cinema in the 1950s. From left to right: Ken Adcock, Mr Culley, a worker for John Sadds, Mr Mason, Mrs Gadson, Fred Norton, Father Christmas not known, Baynon Davis, Mrs Gadson, Mr Collins, Mr Frank Groves, Mr Clay Ratnage, Mr Deacon.

A charabanc outing from the Swan in the early 1950s.

You could leave your front door open

Sometimes for entertainment we used to go to Southend pictures or the arcade. In Wickford you could leave your front door and windows open, you never got anybody breaking in. We went to the cinema in Wickford for ninepence and saw films like *Rhapsody in Blue*, James Mason films, *The Seventh Veil*. Films were black and white then. The manager, Mr John Sauger, used to go round spraying perfume. The film often broke a lot. We now go to the Railway Club each week. It has been going for thirty-five years. On Saturdays they have entertainment; Tuesdays and Thursdays they have bingo.

Doreen Williams

Garden parties

I used to go to the Girls' Friendly Society and to the Kemble's garden parties, where we served the guests with tea and cakes in our little paper caps and aprons. The parties were held to raise money in aid of our society. Mrs Potter used to take the Band of Hope at the Congregational Chapel and she got us to sign the pledge against drinking and smoking. We also enjoyed giving little concerts to other children. Two or three of us would get together and send away for leaflets which had the words of the songs, poems and dialogue on them. We learnt them by heart and would stand on a little platform and perform.

Queenie Thorington

The Quart Pot

We used to go to the cinema in the High Street. It cost a shilling to get in but it was always breaking down and everyone would shout and whistle. When I was a teenager I used to go to the dances in an old tin hut in Jersey Gardens and dance to Bert Easton and his band. There were only three of them: one on piano, one on drums and a lady singer. There used to be a big tree outside the Quart Pot which had a great hole in it and all the kids used to sit in it. When they cut it down it took twelve hours. My husband was in the pub darts team and when they played other pubs we travelled by coach. They ran outings

The Quart Pot darts club, 1936/37. From left to right, back row: A Guiver, J. Smith, G. Keys, L. Fountain, J.Milkhoy coach driver. Middle row: G. Rose, A. Carter (Japper), J. Pedder, L. Flexham, D.Rider, T. Hunt, G Brewer, H. Carter, T. Brown. Front row: A. Carter, R Crackwell, J. Peddler, G. Jupp, H. Hall, J.Worthington, A.Gore.

Wickford Bowls Club during the 1940s. Mr Ted Cox is sixth from left in the middle row.

in charabancs to Margate, Ramsgate, Southend and all over the place. The governor of the pub supplied the sandwiches and we would stop halfway so the women could do a wee in the stinging nettles.

Emily Babbage

Bowling

My husband used to be chairman of Wickford Bowling Club and gave out the prizes.

Joan Cox

We've got one!

As kids, we would go fishing with old bits of rag over to where they were building the Memorial Park. We would hold each end and go to the edge of the water and scoop up sticklebacks and shout out, 'We've got one!' At the Quart Pot they used to play skittles.

Mr Williams

A brick a week

The community hall is where the market was. The Community Association was formed in 1956. Essex County Council put in £15,000 and I think that Basildon Council put in the same, leaving the members to find £5,000. They came up with the idea of collecting sixpence a week – 'a brick a week' was the expression. They raised other money with jumble sales, whist drives, bingo sessions or beetle sessions. It was hard work, apparently. At that time I was not involved in the committee. The hall was finally built in 1964. We have gradually improved it bit by bit and financed the alterations ourselves. The original membership fee was three shillings a year and they would charge a shilling entrance fee. We are completely independent and even pay our own secretary. There are about 860 members now but when I joined there were about 700. The numbers have fluctuated over the years; we have had as many as 1,000. There are eighteen members on the committee: four men and fourteen women. Each club has a representative so they know what is going on. We serve the community in many ways, with keep fit classes, MIND, dancing, chess, short mat bowls, table tennis, fencing and a number of others. We have a bar and serve food. We have a summer dance and one at Halloween. The dancing school were champions at Blackpool in 2003. The couple who started the dancing club used to give lessons. The sequence dancing was one of the original clubs, along with ballroom dancing, fencing and chess. In 2003 we held our fortieth anniversary.

Eddie Noyes

Wickford Community Centre AGM, 20 June 1969.

Old time dancing

I joined the Community Association when it first opened in 1963. We used to watch old time dancing on the television and my husband said, 'That is what I want to do!' Soon after, I saw a notice for the inaugural meeting of the Old Time Dance Club and that's how we started. It cost a shilling. Cathy Maxwell was the instructress and it was marvellous the way she taught us. There were sixty people that first time but only ten knew anything about dancing. As of October 2004, I have been doing old time sequence dancing for forty-one years and still enjoy it. Unfortunately my husband cannot dance any more. It is run by the Association and the leaders have changed over the years. The present ones are David and Josie Griggs. The clubs have committees which make sure everybody is a member and dues are paid. They have a ballroom dance club on Friday. The original clubs at the community hall were the chess club, the fencing club, and the old time sequence dancing. We even used to have the Citizens' Advice in the building.

Doreen Reed

Merley Club

We would go square dancing at Ramsden Bellhouse. It was great fun. There was also a club at Shotgate, open to anyone, where we played darts, table tennis and cards. One of the boy's fathers had an empty cowshed on his smallholding opposite Fred's Woodyard. He said if we cleaned it we could use it. So we smartened it up. It was somewhere to meet and have a chat but unfortunately he sold the land and so we lost our club. Years later, they built the Merley Club there but you had to be eighteen to join.

Mrs Barker

We always had a stocking

At Christmas, my mother would sit on one side of the range opposite a box of wood, newspapers and the Christmas tree. The crackers were always unisex because we did not have much money. Mum would cover our eyes and lift us up and what we touched was ours. I can remember once there was a pair of doll's bootees but I never got them. We always had a stocking which had an apple and shiny penny in it.

Mrs Livermore

Old time dancing at the community hall, probably in the 1960s.

Wickford No1 National Federation of OAPs Association. Among the crowd are, Mr Maddock, Mr. Parker, Mr Smith, Mrs. Lewis, Mrs Watson, Mrs Bristow, Mrs Lyons, MrsWarling, Mrs Webster, Mrs Fulleoid, Mrs Green, Mrs Smith, L. Whiting, Mrs Pale, Mrs Stevens, Mrs Brooks, Lou Ollinggton, Mrs Legget-Smith.

Wrestling

Years ago, the Community Association Centre held wrestling bouts. My brother and I used to put the chairs out but the wrestlers would put the ring up. They put scaffold boards underneath the canvas. They had some good matches: Mick McManus, Big Daddy and Giant Haystacks. I got a lot of their autographs. Sometimes we would go into the Corn Exchange in Chelmsford and watch the wrestling.

Peter Hall

Like father, like sons

My wife Jacqueline and I joined Wickford Air Training Corps in 1964 as civilian instructors. The ATC started during the war and we drilled and had weapon training. I went up in Chipmunks at Marshals in Cambridge, then I did gliding at Debden. While I was there, in 1967, they were making the *Battle of Britain* film and that is what started my interest in flying history. I was in the ATC 1474 Squadron and so were my two sons. Darren was promoted to sergeant and is now a gunner and does re-enactments of the Second World War with the Living History Group. They did a re-enactment in front of Prince Michael of Kent at Chatham Docks, Kent. Sammy, my other son, is into martial arts and music.

Trevor Williams

Let him play

Mr Newman was the head at Nevendon School and ran the football team. There were not many pupils and so if you were interested and could kick a ball, you were in. The first game I ever played was against Stock School in 1932, when I was nine and they were fourteen. They had rugby tackle people, like the Keelings. In that game I touched the ball twelve times and one of them was the kick-off and the rest was after they had scored a goal. I played centre forward but after that I always played as a right-winger. When Craylands School first opened in 1934 I played for them. They were a bit different to Nevendon School as you had to have a trial. Most of the games were on Saturday morning at Jones Memorial Ground. They had a grandstand and used to sell Nelson cakes for a penny. They were lovely.

Some games we knew we were going to win, like when we played the Sacred Heart Convent School. In 1947 I played as a winger for Wickford Football Club. I remember George Horn, who was a good player and went on to play for a number of clubs in the north of England. In those days, Laurie Gunn used to play in goal. Another player I remember was Frankie Thorington, who was a foreman at Carter and Ward. The Wickford Football Club used to hold an annual dance at Runwell Village Hall. Apart from the Wickford team there was also the Darby Rovers. My brother played for them and one day I was watching when the captain, Thomson, said, 'We are one short, let him play', and he pointed to me. 'At least he'll be nuisance value.' That was my first match with them.

Mr Nightingale

Wickford Football Club, 1936.

Anything with a ball

The first recorded Wickford cricket match was in 1887. I first played for them in 1947 when Bill Timpson, who was a schoolteacher at Brentwood School, took me down to the ground to play in an under-fifteens game against a school. Michael Bear, who later played for Essex, was playing against us then. The Wickford club in those days was a bit of a closed shop and after the match I did not hear any more for a while. After that, I played for Runwell Hospital for a few years. Dick Patmore was the president of Wickford Cricket Club and also a founder member, with Franklin the local butcher and two or three others. He also captained the Wickford team along with the Essex club on the ground side. The ground was originally behind the Castle pub where the Aldi supermarket is

now. It then moved to Franklin's Field, which is now the roundabout, then to its current location off Swan Lane, which was owned by Dick Patmore, who bequeathed it to his daughter Madeline, who then left it in trust to the club.

One of the leading lights in the twenties was Maurice Nichols, who started playing for Wickford then transferred to Essex Cricket Club and also played for England. In my time we had some good players like the Mayes brothers and the Maplesons. Stan Coates was captain and there were only a first and second eleven for Saturdays and Sundays. Now there are four elevens on a Saturday and two on Sundays. Years ago, fixtures were arranged locally with teams of similar standing and were transported to matches by horse and cart. In those days it depended on your ability and

WICKFORD CC 1966
Trevor Crook, Harold Bohanon, Peter Madams, Peter Matthews,
Peter Bryant, George Scoble, Alan Goddard, Bert Bury, Stan Coates
Bobby Mayes, Lester Crook.

Wickford Cricket Club 1966.

social standing whether they let you play. In the seventies, the leagues started with promotions and relegations.

What attracted me to cricket in the first place was that a ball was involved. I also played football, tennis and hockey. At school, tennis is difficult because at most only four can play; with cricket, you need to mow a strip and put stumps in; but with football you throw some coats down and you have twenty-two boys playing. I originally started playing football with Runwell Youth Centre, which was run by Stan Caldwell, and we met in the Rectory Hall just at the top of Church End Lane. It was a wooden hut and one night a gale was blowing outside while we were playing snooker and table tennis and suddenly there was this tremendous roar and a tree crashed across the roof. Luckily nobody was hurt. After that, in 1949, they built a permanent brick youth centre round the corner in Church End Lane, which has now been demolished and replaced with houses. I played an exhibition table tennis match with Stan Caldwell the night they opened it. He taught us table tennis, boxing and ran the football team. Occasionally I used to spar with Terry Dove, who later played in goal for Arsenal Reserves. I was also lucky enough to play table tennis against Victor Borna in an exhibition match on finals night at the Rotary Hoes at West Horndon.

Stan Caldwell used to get youth football teams over from Germany to play against Runwell Youth Club at the Manor Ground in Southend Road. Several players went on to play for professional clubs. Henry and Terry Dove both went to Arsenal. Harry Warren invited me to play for Southend for a season in the reserves but I did not make the grade and went from there to Clacton in the Eastern Counties League. After that, I played for Battlesbridge for about nine years, which was a very enjoyable time.

I played hockey for Wickford men's and mixed teams. My wife Anne also played, as did my mother-in-law, Pearl Haddon. She actually played a couple of games after reaching sixty. Miss Amos, one of our teachers, also played hockey. It seemed funny as she once sent me for the cane and Mr Rose the headmaster said, 'If Miss Amos sent you, you must deserve it.'

Alan Goddard

I was out first ball

Although I am a vice-president of Wickford Cricket Club I have only played cricket there once, it was the tennis club v. cricket club friendly. I was out first ball and when I was fielding, I dropped a catch. My daughter still remembers it. The ground slopes a bit from side to side across the wicket. The ground is off Swan Lane and Runwell Road and was part of Stilemans Farm which Dick Patmore purchased in 1906. The ground included three tennis courts on the edge of the cricket boundary and the cricket and tennis pavilions. I understand that that they used to play on Franklins Field fronting Southend Road. In 1955 Dick Patmore's daughter Madeline leased the ground to the representatives of the cricket and tennis clubs. In 1988 a meeting was held at the Windmill public house in South Hanningfield and the ground was transferred to trustees. I was one of the trustees along with Chick Thomas, Pat Colling and Alan Finch. Madeline died in 1999 and the ground is permanently styled the Dick Patmore Memorial Sports Ground, as she wished. Madeline and her cousin George Patmore always visited the ground until they got too elderly. George was for a long time president of the club and Madeline played tennis and is listed as the 1936 Ladies' Singles Champion. Out of season, the ground was used to play hockey, until the advent of the preferred Astroturf pitches elsewhere. The cricket pitch was overseen at one time by Jack Mayes and then later by Pearl's husband, Wallace Haddon. On the ground is an old cricket horse-drawn roller commemorat-

Above: The roller dedicated to Madeline Patmore at the sports ground.

Below: Wickford's ladies' hockey team, 1949. Mary Cockie is second from left in the back row.

ing Madeline. When she was young, she used its shafts as a swing.

Reg Iles

The Dirty Ducks

In 1941 I joined the Wickford ladies' hockey team. There was also a men's team which was depleted during the war but once it was over they got into full swing. There was also a mixed team. We played on the cricket field in so-called friendly matches with the Billericay ladies. Shins got a beating on both sides. We met at the White Swan public house and were called the White Swans and had a white swan on our navy blue shorts. The Billericay team called us the Dirty Ducks. When my friend Pearl raised her hockey stick to hit the ball, everybody cringed. If I tackled somebody and they got past me they came up against Pearl and that was their lot! I only once went into the pub with the team because, as a teacher, it was just not done, especially if you were a woman.

Mary Cockie (Miss Amos)

Twenty-two sticks

I played hockey for Wickford from 1964 to 1988 and was chairman and at one time treasurer. I still play for Brentwood. I started playing while I was in the RAF. One week we would play football, the next rugby. One Wednesday they issued us with twenty-two sticks and a hard ball and said, 'You're playing hockey.' Only a few of the guys had played at school; the rest knew nothing about it and so we hit everything. I enjoyed it and played football as well. When I came out of the forces I started playing football for STC and then took up hockey again. I played when we were in Kent and then when we moved here in 1964 we wanted to continue fencing, tennis, hockey and bridge. We found all four here in Wickford. We joined Wickford Tennis Club and one of the club officials, Mrs Copeman, used to arrange all the matches when we went along on a Sunday. I used to play with Alan Goddard and would pass him the ball and he would score. He was a real good all-rounder. When we went for a corner and charged out from behind the line, David Mead would say, 'I'll get him and you get that one!'

Charles Read

Wickford's Mixed Hockey Club during the 1960s. From left to right, back row: Wallace Haddon, Ned, Alan Goddard, Stan Cokes, Chick Thomas, Bruce Haddon, Peter Woodward. Front row: Brenda Spurling, Anne Haddon, Pearl Haddon, Maureen Bryden, Beryl Spencer, Jackie Spiller. The team were unbeaten for two seasons.

I got a green belt

When I was seventeen I started going to judo at Wickford Community Centre, where George Stubbings was the tutor. I got a green belt. I am not sure if the club in Wickford closed or I learned to drive; however, I started going to judo in Maldon.

Joyce Ward

Girls' Training Corps

There was an organisation for the boys – the ATC – and we also had one for the girls called the Girls' Training Corps (GTC). Miss Saltwell, the headmistress of the junior school, was the Commandant and I was her deputy. Two evenings a week the girls would turn up for various classes. We persuaded some members

The Judo Club warming up. Joyce Ward is on the left, aged seventeen.

The Girls' Training Corps in 1944. Mary Cockie is third from left in the front row.

of staff at the school to teach them such skills as cookery and practical subjects, including map-reading. Every month we had a church parade at St Catherine's. We would line up and get into ranks at the junior school in Market Road and then march all the way through the town up to the church. Miss Saltwell was quite a small woman and she would start off like a greyhound, leaving me struggling to keep up, especially up the hills. By the time we got to the church we were screaming for mercy. Some of the girls are still around.

Mary Cockie (Miss Amos)

All week it rained

During the war I belonged to the Girls' Training Corps and Miss Amos ran it. They trained us for the services. If the war had continued I would have gone in the WAAF. We drilled and went to camp at West Bergholt in Colchester, sleeping in Bell tents. We had a rota for cooking and washing up and we were allowed into Colchester a couple of nights. All week it rained. I never went camping again.

Doreen Williams

We were never afraid

After I left school at fourteen I joined the Junior Girls' Training Corps and the Runwell Youth Club where they held dances and played table tennis. I would walk there with my friend from the other side of Wickford in the blackout; we were never afraid.

Shirley Dines

Air Training Corps

I was in the ATC and the army cadets used to be our rivals, it was good fun. We played them at football, which we mostly won, and boxing matches, which was a different story as we were gentlemen. I played for the Essex ATC

against various counties. I remember playing Kent and thrashing them 6-1. I played cricket for the works team; they put me in last.

Peter Hall

Tennis tournament

When they had their local shows we would have a tennis tournament. There was all the noise of the fair engines and people milling about but because Pearl was deaf she just plodded on. She stood at the net and banged everything that came near her while I was dashing about at the back, clearing anything that passed her. We did not have leagues in those days but ran tournaments where your partner was picked out of a hat, so it was the luck of the draw. Pearl and I won the doubles a number of times but I never managed to beat her at singles. Rene Fox, Pearl and I were normally in the finals. I could never beat either of them.

Mary Cockie (Miss Amos)

On the committee

I joined Wickford Lawn Tennis Club in April 1959. In those days we only played from April to the end of September. After that, the hockey club used the pavilion and ground during the winter. The tennis club member-ship fee for the summer was three guineas. My membership was vetted by Rene Fox, the then secretary. All the other committee members were playing away. In 1960 Joyce Reynolds and I won the finals of the mixed doubles. It was handicapped as we were playing two of the top younger players, Tommy Caldwell and Margaret Dale. Pearl Haddon was then the top lady player. Her son-in-law Alan Goddard and Tommy Caldwell were the top pair of young chaps. Many of the tennis players also played hockey, including Pearl Haddon and Mary Cockie. The three tennis courts are at the edge

Brookfield cricket field in the 1930s.

of the cricket outfield and are shown on the 1910 Ordnance Survey sheet. In January 1960 the AGM was held in the Swan public house and Mr Copeman, the tennis club treasurer, was retiring. I was voted in to replace him and I served as honorary treasurer for forty-one years. The chairman at that time was Geoff Gower, the secretary was Margaret Dale, and Pearl Haddon, her son Bruce and son-in-law Alan Goddard were the other members of the committee. A long-serving committee member was Ken Bowser, who was elected as secretary in 1961 and later was for many years our chairman. Our long-serving secretary is Sandra Ellis. Ken Bowser was president for a time and I now have that honour.

Ron Iles

Brookfield

One field on our farm was a cricket field called Brookfield; the Manor Cricket Club used it. It is all factories now.

Joan Cox

Carnival Queen

Years ago one of my sisters was Carnival Queen and my mum stood at the back of the crowd cheering her on down the High Street.

Fred Smith

Wickford Car Club

I was seventeen when I joined Wickford Car Club and my car became my hobby. At weekends I would either be fixing it or racing it. The club was started by Jim Orr and Dan Cornwall. We met at the Wickford Community Centre and I kept my sports car and Morris 8 Tourer going. With my Dad's help I rebuilt both of those: he supplied some of the knowledge and I did the hands-on bit. The wheel arches were made of five Castrol tins. I took a gearbox out of the Ford car and put it all back with Dad's advice. After I had repaired it I went out but the gears would not change properly. When I got back I told Dad. He bent down and picked up a bit of metal and held it up. 'I don't know if you recognise this?' I said, 'What's that then?' He replied, 'It could help you to change your gears. It's a synchroniser.' So another weekend was spent taking the gearbox out, putting the bit in and putting it all back together. The club held rallies and we drove round country lanes. We also

Wickford Car Club.

exchanged information on different cars. The club is still going but now meets in the Fox and Hounds at Downham.

Joyce Ward

Puss In Boots

The carnivals in Wickford were wonderful and in particular I remember the Mala School of Dancing. Miss Upton was their principal and played Puss in Boots on the back of the coal lorry. My sister and I desperately wanted to go to dancing classes but could not afford it. There used to be a great marquee filled with cakes and although I was frightened of wasps I could not resist the great big meringues. Everybody joined in,

all the local businessmen. Carter and Ward, the builders, used their big lorries and we would get on them and pretend we could tap dance.

Mrs Livermore

Year of the Child

Wickford holds a carnival each year and during the Year of the Child we had this big rocket upon which Miriam, one of the helpers, had written a large notice which said 'A Play Space for Every Child.' It caught the telephone wires and brought them down and I don't think parts of Wickford had telephones for a week.

Beryl Abbot

Five of Wickford's Carnival Queens.

The Wickford Clinic Mothers' Club
won first prize in the 1967 carnival.

Wearing fancy dress for the
Coronation of George V in 1937.
Joan Cox is second from the left.

Wickford Horticultural Club Dinner, 1948. George Mead is second from right.

Wickford Horticultural Society

In 1948 my father helped to form the Wickford Horticultural Society and became its first chairman. My intense interest in gardening stemmed from my father and I eventually joined the society. For twenty-five years I was show manager and became chairman in 1998. I retired from the position in 2004. The Horticultural Society has been going for fifty-six years and is still going strong with 109 members.

William Mead

Girl Guides, Brownies and Rainbows

My daughter and I went to Brownsea Island to see where Scouting and Guiding was born. The births of the organisations took place in 1907 and 1909 respectively. Wickford must have been very forward-looking because Girl Guiding started in 1919 when Phyllis Booth started up the 1st Wickford Brownies in St Catherine's church hall. They now meet in Mount Road. From those small beginnings there are now over 250 Rainbows, Brownies and Girl Guides in Wickford. The Rainbows are aged from five to seven, the Brownies from seven to ten and the Girl Guides from ten to fourteen. You can become a Ranger at fourteen and you can also go on to train as a leader. Wickford is now split into east and west. Unfortunately, as leaders retire, units merge and get smaller, that is why the pack numbers don't run consecutively. Some Brownies share the same venues as the Girl Guides.

I was a Guide and Brownie in London and when my daughter was old enough she became a Guide here in Wickford. Eleven years ago I asked the leader if they needed any assistance and she replied yes. For the first year I was a mum helper and then the leader was promoted at work and could not do the job any more and suggested I took over. I told her that I would need help. She said she thought it would have to close. Then one night I got a telephone call from Glynis Wright, who said her daughter was in tears because she thought we were going to close and so we decided to keep the group going. We started our training with the 1st Wickford. I became qualified but as Glynis had been a Queen's Guide we decided that she would be the leader and I would be her assistant. It works out well because she is good with finances and administration. I am good at planning. Some of the past leaders were Molly Dollman, Shirley Phipps and Lilian Irvine. There are two District Commissioners: Lyn Campbell, who runs Wickford West, and Lynne Vine, who runs Wickford East.

We give the girls the opportunity to be selected for World Jamborees and as they are our ambassadors they are selected for their qualities. Wickford has done exceptionally well sending girls on jamborees. Sarah Campbell recently went to Canada. We raised £1,400 for her but she had to get involved with raising the money. One year my daughter Carla was selected and went to New Zealand.

Joyce Ward

Phyllis Booth, who started the 1st Wickford Brownies in 1919.

Joyce Ward and her daughter Carla at Brownsea Island, the birthplace of Scouting and Guiding.

Jubilee

I joined the Brownies and was involved in the procession of decorated vehicles for Queen Mary and King George V's Jubilee.

Christine Hoad (*née* Franklin)

Good fun

I was in the Guides during the thirties. I thought it was good fun.

Joan Cox

The night of the hurricane

I took over the 1st Wickford and Janette Walker asked me to go away for a long week-end to Harlow with a dozen girls. It was the night of the hurricane. We pitched the tents by the side of a river and the warden came along and warned us that the weather was going to be bad. We laughed and said we were Guides, we would be fine. That night it howled and blew. In the next tent we heard the girls screaming with laughter. Suddenly we heard an almighty scream and we shot out to find one of the tents was ripped from one end to the other. We thought they had been larking about and ordered one to go in one tent and the other to go in another and their luggage had to come in with us.

Joyce Ward

Scouts in a chicken shed

The Scouts were started in Wickford in 1928 by Reg Payne. He had been a Chief Petty

Joan Cox in her Guide uniform in the 1930s.

Joan Cox today.

Officer in the Royal Navy Volunteer Reserve in the First World War and when the Second World War started he was called up. The Scouts used to meet in a chicken shed in Ethelred Gardens. During the Second World War most of the leaders joined up and so, to overcome this shortage, the 1st Runwell and the Stock Scouts joined forces and were run by a man called Padwick, who was the head gardener of Downham Grange. Soon after I was demobbed I started to run the 1st Runwell and Stock Scouts under Reg Payne. The meetings were still held in the chicken shed but it was so crowded that we held them outside, in the orchard, unless it rained.

Unfortunately the land was sold to Sylver Carter. I then left to start the 1st Downham Scout Group and they met in the old barn at Downham Grange, which was owned by Mrs Keddie. She lost three sons in the Second World War. A number of the boys came from the Hanningfields and when the reservoir was built they left. At twenty-eight I was made Assistant District Commissioner for Billericay

Above: Girl Guides and Brownies marching down Southend Road in the early days.

Below: Norman Simmons, District Commissioner.

and Wickford District. After two years I was made up to District Commissioner and served for twenty years, retiring at forty-five. At one time there were ten or twelve groups in the district but that was when there was a lot more interest than there is today. Most of the Duke of Edinburgh Awards are based on things the Scouts do.

My most frightening moment was when I took a group down to Deal and camped on the edge of a cliff. It was the scariest two weeks of my life as I tried to keep the boys away from the edge. We had help from local businesses, in particular Sid Sutton of Wickford Store, who never let us down.

Norman Simmons

Never take your eye off the ball

I was just soaked in sport and watched cricket and football during my childhood in Ascot, where my father and I would sit under a line of lime trees and watch the matches. My mum would come along with a picnic of strawberries dipped in sugar or radishes dipped in salt. I'll never forget one football match. I was standing there looking around, a little bit bored as the match had hit a quiet spot, when suddenly this ball hit me smack between the shoulders and I fell flat on my face. My dad picked me up out of the mud and said, 'Never take your eye off the ball.'

Mary Cockie (Miss Amos)

Fencing

The Wickford Fencing Club started in Beauchamps School in 1962 as an evening class. Norman Sharp was the instructor then and when the Community Centre opened in 1963 we applied and got in. We meet on Tuesday nights. Our fencing club is so popular that we have a waiting list. At the moment there are more adults than youngsters but it is a sport for all ages. Even older people come along and learn the basics. It's a good way to keep fit. When I was young in London and my husband Charles was in the RAF, I wanted something to do of an evening, either judo or fencing. There was a course in fencing at Glyn Road School, off the Homerton High Street, and I joined. When Charles got out of the Air Force he came along with me and we have been fencing ever since. Charles still teaches and fences competitively although I cannot any more because I've got arthritis.

Pat Read

Wickford Fencing Club

When a beginner comes into the club I get him or her kitted up. I give them an elementary lesson and can tell within seconds whether they are going to make a fencer. It is hand, foot and eye coordination. We have run an annual competition for eighteen years as well as county and other events. There are three types of weapons: the foil, the sabre and the épée. We started doing weekend courses at Bisham Abbey, the National Sports Centre in Marlow, Bucks, a weekend of non-stop fencing. It was suggested that we did some coaching and so we both started the coaching course which ran over a year. It involved three weekends and at the end of it we hoped to take the Elementary Coaching Certificate. When the course finished I was told I could take the exam as I had a good chance of passing but Pat was told, 'We don't think you will pass but you can take it if you want to.' I failed and Pat passed. I had to take it again six months later. I am qualified to teach the three weapons. The foil is the elementary training weapon but is a competitive weapon. When you press the tip a circuit is made so that when you hit the target area a coloured light comes up but other hits come up white and do not score. Only the body is the target.

Pat and Charles Read showing their fencing skills.

Ladies' Club Championship. From left to right, back row: Pat Read, Jan Wheatley, Florence Coyne, -?-, Barbara Pountney, Mary Boling. Front row: Bryony Ackland, Sally Wakeling.

The épée is a slightly heavier sword and was the duelling weapon years ago. You can score a hit on any part of the body. The sabre is the cavalry weapon of cut and thrust.

There are county, regional and national competitions. Our three boys took it up and we went out as a family. My youngest son started fencing when he was five and when he was nine he qualified for his first national final. He fenced until he was thirteen, when he won both the Slough and Basildon Open. Neil Ashdown, who fenced for England in the 1994 Commonwealth Games, was a member of our club until he was twelve. Pat fenced in Southend's Open Foil in 1970. I was walking round the sports hall with the boys while she fenced in the final. In 1985 she won the Essex Open Foil ladies' team championship.

I had one bad accident when I nearly killed a friend of mine. He came at me with a very fast attack, I parried and hit him but the blade broke. I saw it vanish under his bib. I looked at my broken foil and saw it was bloodstained. He had a great puncture in his neck and blood was running down his jacket. We got to hospital, where the doctor said, 'You re the luckiest person alive – another fraction of an inch and you would be dead.' He was back fencing two weeks later.

Charles Read

seven

Wickford in Uniform

Above: A group of volunteer friends off to Kingston Barracks at the start of the First World War. Mr Amos is second from left.

Below: Some of the same friends in uniform, 1915. Mr Amos is in the second row, extreme right.

First World War

Queenie Thorington at the age of one, in the arms of her uncle, William Bewers Jnr, with Mrs Adda Mercy Carter (*née* Bewers) and her grandfather, William Bewers, outside Runwick Cottage in Runwell Road.

He never came home

I was four when the First World War started and eight when it finished. I can remember standing at our gate and seeing all the soldiers marching by with mules pulling the guns along. I stood there for ages and ages and all the time these soldiers were going by. Some waved and smiled. I was looking for my Uncle Bob but I could not see him. They were going up Runwell Road towards the church. As a child I thought it was the whole British Army. There were loads of horses and in those days they did not have lorries and had to march miles. My Uncle Bob went missing in France. Somebody said they had seen him on a stretcher being carried out of the trenches and that only his legs were injured. We were very hopeful but he never came home. Uncle Will was on a submarine and was reported missing. We learned later that he had been sunk and drowned.

The authorities came round and decided we had to have two soldiers billeted on us. All us children crowded into one bedroom. The soldiers were from the Scottish Regiment and the Middlesex Regiment and were very respectful. After the war I travelled up to London on my own and stayed with one of the soldier's families in their flat up in Peckham, London. My mother took me to the station and spoke to the guard, who put me on a little armchair seat. He put me off at Liverpool Street and I was glad to see the soldier and his family waiting at the barrier. He got hold of me and lifted me over the rail. I stayed for a week and remember there was a pub across the road called the Nelson and another called the Victory. We went to Hyde Park, the Zoo and places like that.

My father went away during the war but he was not healthy enough to go into the Army so they sent him to the docks: sometimes it was Tilbury docks, sometimes it was Dartford. He was a carpenter and joiner and when the ships came in he helped to turn them into troop ships and they kept him there even when the war finished.

Queenie Thorington

They sent him back three times

My father got wounded in the First World War. They patched him up and sent him back three times and then finally he was badly gassed and was taken prisoner. It was as a result of the gassing that he developed TB and died at forty-eight.

Mary Cockie (Miss Amos)

Sergeant Amos and his wife relaxing on leave, 1917.

Zeppelin

I saw the Zeppelin come down over Burstead. My mother took me out of my cot and held me as it came over Wickford and it looked as if it was going to come down at any time. I think they got me out for safety. There were flames in the sky and by the time it had gone over us, it had come down. The next day we went over to Burstead. I cannot remember how we got there but I can remember all the twisted girders lying on the ground.

Later on, a German Gotha plane came down between the river and London Road while I was at school and after school all the children went down to see it. We just stood and stared. What I remember most was the terrible smell of the bodies. When we came away I got to the river bridge and was sick.

Queenie Thorington

Ten bob a week

My Uncle Johnny was only eighteen when he joined up for the First World War. He was only out in France two days when Nan got a telegram to say that he had been killed. She got ten bob a week. It was not much for a life, although in those days you could get a lot for ten bob. You could buy half a pound of margarine for twopence. You could take your cup and get twopence of mustard pickle. The shopkeeper would bring out a big jar and scoop it out. Five pounds of potatoes was only sixpence, a loaf of bread was about twopence. You could go round the butcher's and get a piece of beef for six shillings. Mum would give me a note for the butcher which said, 'A piece of salt beef and not all end.' My dad would say, 'If you bring back all end, you can take it back.'

Doris Orton

Food shortages

We could not get a lot of things, like butter, and my mother hated the margarine so she used to take the cream off the milk and shake it and shake it until it turned into butter. It used to come out white. The margarine was terrible and we could not stand it without jam. We did have ration books.

Queenie Thorington

Sunk in both wars

My uncle was in the Merchant Navy for thirty years and was sunk in both wars. When he arrived in port he would send a telegram and frighten the life out of my mother because normally a telegram meant bad news.

John Dowman

He had his jaw shot away

My father was in the First World War and had his jaw shot away. When he came home and told me tales about the war I found them difficult to believe, especially how they used to dig jam out of the mud.

Norman Simmons

Royal Flying Corps

My father, Albert Blackburn, was a rubber planter in Malaya and when the First World War started he came home and joined up. At first, he was a lieutenant in the Observer Corps and went up in balloons over the trenches directing artillery fire. He was lucky as most did not survive long. He then transferred to the Royal Flying Corps and flew Sopwith Camels. They were byplanes. Like most of the men that came back he did not talk about it; they saw too much horror. After the war he went back to his plantation and stayed there until his first wife died. He was there when the market collapsed in the thirties and lost everything.

Joan Blackburn

Bombed and shelled

My grandfather, Thomas Dines, captained a barge which took supplies out to Belgium and France during the First World War and brought back empty ammunition cases. He got bombed and shelled a number of times.

Shirley Dines

Second World War

Rockets and doodlebugs

The war was horrible. Living in a shelter for years on end. We had an indoor one which was like a big metal table; I think they were called Morrison shelters. When we moved to a bigger house at the top of Bruce Grove we had an Anderson shelter dug into the ground. It had bunk beds and we all slept and played cards in it. When there was a raid the first one out was the dog. We watched loads of air fights and the searchlights used to pick out the enemy planes. I remember the direct hit up Rectory Road. The rockets and doodlebugs used to be really terrifying. You never heard the rockets until they exploded. With the doodlebugs, first you heard this terrible droning noise then it stopped and you waited for the explosion. We got blasted out and moved to another house down the road. I can remember someone shouting, 'Anyone in, anyone in?' We were all fast asleep in the same room and didn't hear a thing. When we looked, we had no front door or windows. We just got used to it, it was part of life.

We used to walk up as far as the tank traps, which were great big ditches about the size of a room and sloping down on one side. They were built in case of an invasion, to trap enemy tanks. Shotgate was surrounded by tank traps and blockhouses. They are listed buildings now.

Yvonne Wilkinson

Swirling kilts up the High Street

At the beginning of the war nothing much seemed to happen, then all of a sudden the village was swarming with the Black Watch and the Highland Light Infantry billeted in church halls and any spare accommodation ready for returning to France. It was strange to hear bagpipes followed by platoons of swirling kilts marching up the High Street.

No foreign fruits were imported during the war. There was the big campaign to Dig for Victory, when every patch of garden was dug up, the backs and the fronts. We dug a big hole in the back garden to put in our Anderson shelter, a corrugated metal building into which we disappeared each time the siren sounded to warn us of the German bombers which were trying to destroy London. We were on the direct course to their targets and suffered quite a lot of damage. I do not know how our parents kept sane.

Christine Hoad (*née* Franklin)

Gas masks

The war started when I was seventeen. I was frightened out of my life. My mum had a fish shop in Upton Park which she let so we could move to Cherrydown Avenue in Chingford because she thought it would be safer. On 3 September 1939 we were gathered round the radio at eleven o'clock waiting for Chamberlain to speak. We all went silent as he said we were at war with Germany. My mum did no more than get the gas masks. 'Put them on,' she ordered. My brother was still a baby and had a box one. She put him in it and then she pulled out the great big sideboard.

'Get behind there,' she commanded. There we all sat behind this great big sideboard, with our gas masks on, while she stood over us. I remember thinking, 'Oh my God, I wonder how long this is going to go on.' Then the all-clear went and frightened me even more. My mum said, 'Come on, take your gas masks off.'

Doris Orton

Our gas was cut off

When the war first started, they dropped bombs over Corringham and cut off all our gas. We had electric light but we did not have an electric cooker. When my husband came home on leave, he went straight to Mayes in Wickford and bought a little coal Kitchener which he fitted in the fireplace. I always had a big saucepan of water boiling on it. There was an oven and I would cook rice puddings and things like that for the kids. When my husband came

The bomb dropped on the cricket grounds of Runwell Hospital in November 1941.

home on leave, I would use up all my meat and cheese coupons on him. Sometimes the butcher would make up the ration with sausages, which were not on ration but you could only get two because everybody wanted them. He also had suet which he would cut up.

Queenie Thorington

If it had your name on it

I was on the milk round with my dad and Mr Morrell came out and told us that war had been declared and he invited us in for a cup of coffee. All the men were sitting round talking about it and that night the siren went off but luckily it was only a practice one. One day I remember coming home with oil spots on me that had drifted over from the oil refinery. A little while later I remember my mother whispering to me that France had fallen. I realised what it meant and was frightened. One Sunday during the Battle of Britain I remember seeing my first Spitfire spinning down out of the sky on fire and then the parachute opened. Dr Cameron raced towards the crash followed by all the kids on bikes but my mother would not let me go. The pilot had got one of his boots trapped, which delayed him getting out. My aunt found the boot on the farm. Unfortunately the pilot died.

We were going to have our photos taken in the garden but every time we went out a plane came over and we had to rush in. The first time a doodlebug came over I was in bed. I heard a crash but I did not take any notice. Next morning when dad returned from his milk round he put his head round the door and said, 'That was a pilotless plane last night, the soldiers have just told me.' I can remember being afraid. There was the one that landed in the London Road. After that I used to sleep all through the night. I thought, if it has my name on it, that's it.

Shirley Dines

A lot of them stayed

One night I saw a searchlight catch a German plane in the lights and saw him drop a parachute mine, which we followed down in the beam. A lot of people who got bombed out in the London area came to live in Wickford and were allocated the houses in Wick Drive. A lot of them stayed. One of the girls married one of the chaps I went to school with.

Peter Hall

Sweets and chocolate

The Army used to park their lorries all the way down Crouch Road. They had commandeered No. 71 Southend Road, which was on the brow of the hill and ideal to see the surrounding countryside. We used to have rides on their vehicles and go up to the house, where they would give us sweets and chocolate. Miss Elmore still lives there. They left their vehicles in the field at the bottom but had to be careful because it got flooded. There is the roundabout there now, by the garage.

Barrie Adcock

Let's get out of here

I was born in East London, Canning Town, on 17 July 1917. In 1940 the bombing was bad round the docks and loads of people got killed. We were worried it might be our turn next. My brother-in-law said, 'Let's get out of here' and so we loaded the furniture on his lorry and drove down to Wickford. We came to Cedar Avenue, found an empty bungalow and squatted. The three families slept on the floor. The people who owned the property never came back. Eventually the council took it over.

Mr Spindler

Back to the Valleys

I was up in Cardiff at the start of the war, receiving our packet of bombs. Our landlady had a husband and son. There were three of us girl students and she would not leave us in the same room as the men. Then one night a bomb dropped nearby and the roof caved in and the windows were blown out. The door was found in the local cemetery. After that we did not see the landlady for dust. She went back up to her mum in the Valleys.

Mary Cockie (Miss Amos)

Bombed out

My husband built us an Anderson shelter before he went away. It had earth and turf over the top, which made it safe from shrapnel but not from a direct hit. The only trouble was, it leaked and Dad had to keep pumping it out. We had beds and my husband made a cot which was not as wide as a normal one. At first the bombs and guns did not wake Jill, my daughter, but as she got older she got frightened so we put cushions under the bed and crawled under it. One day I looked out the window and saw my rather bedraggled sister and family coming up the path. She lived in Manor Park and had been bombed out. She was really shattered and so they went down the shelter while we slept indoors. As the war went on and things got worse, we all squeezed into the shelter except the men and my mother-in-law.

Queenie Thorington

Grandad went back to bed

Mum used to put me under the table while she dressed my brother in his siren suit, then she dressed me before we went down the shelter. My brother had a gas mask but I did not. Later, when there was an air raid, grandad would get us all out of bed and shepherd us down the shelter and then go back to bed.

Jackie Joyce

We all hit the ground

The raids seemed to go on for months and I remember going down the Anderson shelter in Ilford in 1941. On 7 September 1940 I saw a big orange glow in the sky and thought they had hit Beckton Gas Works but it was the docks in London. During one daylight raid there was an enormous series of bangs and I thought they had hit the school opposite but I realised that a mobile gun had pulled up outside our house. The school was untouched. After that experience, we packed up and came to Wickford. In 1944 I was in the Scouts and camping near Hertford when a doodlebug's motor suddenly cut out overhead and we all hit the ground. I remember breathing a sigh of relief when I saw a great plum of smoke in the distance. When the siren went off, Mum would get us up and herd us into the hall as we did not have a shelter. We watched the doodlebugs fly almost straight down Church End Lane.

Alan Goddard

The only casualty was my dad's bike

A V2 rocket fell at the back of us, taking off half the roof. Workmen came from Rayleigh and tied tarpaulin over the roof and reglazed the windows. When my dad came home from the Army he went out to his shed to get his bike but found it in bits. It was all battered and bent, a war casualty. Not to be outdone, he straightened it out and rode it for years with a wooden peg in the saddle to keep it square. I have seen him ride home from work on a burst tyre with a piece of rope tied round the wheel. At Battlesbridge, on the river, there were great lockgates which had big round hollow concrete slabs on each bank which could be blown if there was an invasion.

Mr Barker

Lucky to be alive

In September 1940, at about 9 p.m., my uncle, aunt and I went for a walk and got to Woolshots Road, when we heard the guns firing in the distance and looking up we saw the search-lights. As the raid built up, we decided to catch the bus home and I sat amidships on the left hand side. We just got to where Turpin's Tyres is now when the bombs rained down and the bus bounced up and down as people screamed out in fear. We got out at Wickford Broadway and the whole area was alight with incendiary bombs. Herbert English ran out with a bucket of sand, trying to put them out. My aunt got hysterical when she saw smoke rising behind the Co-op and thought it was her house in Elm Road on fire. In fact it was next door. When we got home, we found an incendiary bomb had gone through the roof next door and burnt itself out in the fireplace.

On 2 October 1940, my two cousins, named Bolden, came round. We already had relations staying with us from Tilbury, which had been badly bombed. That night we were sleeping on the floor in the front room when a parachute mine landed about 300 metres up the road, killing Mr and Mrs Pratt and their daughter Molly. Our front window blew in and smothered us in broken glass. Amazingly, none of us was injured. Aunt Rose looked like Al Jolson as she got covered in soot.

John Dowman

We could not take a chance

During the war I was teaching in the Market Road building. The shelters were down both sides and sometimes we were in them all day. Directly the siren went, the children formed an orderly queue and trooped out room by room in silence, with their books and their gas masks. Sometimes it was a false alarm but we could not take a chance. The toilet was a bucket in the corner with a curtain round it. During those days, how we ever taught them anything was a miracle. We were lucky, as the school did not sustain any damage. Opposite us were the infants and juniors, they became overcrowded and so some came to us. We would see a crocodile of little ones coming across the road. Mr Rose, the head, would say, 'The PBI (poor blessed infants) are on their way.'

Mary Cockie (Miss Amos)

Parachute silk

The fire brigade in those days had to wait until the police turned up before they could do anything. My dad, who was a fireman, said that as they went up Swan Lane to go to the Pratts' house, the people that got killed with the landmine, it was a wonder that they did not have their heads cut off because of the hanging wires across the road. In our garden we found parachute silk from the landmine. I wound it up and made dishcloths. My dad got a piece of the mine and made three rings out of it. There was no public shelter in Wickford so when the siren went we hurried home.

Doreen Williams

Sandbags

The fire brigade used to park on the front-age of Kershaw's. We lived opposite on Halls Corner, where my parents had a greengrocer's. We held open the sandbags for the men to fill for the shelter in front. The fire station later moved to the London Road, opposite Bolton's, not far from the cycle shop.

Christine Hoad (née Franklin)

The first new fire appliance, a Commer Carmichael, in 1945. Christine Hoad's father, Jack Franklin, is in the centre, wearing the flat hat. His son is by his side.

Half and half

During the first few months of the war I occasionally stopped with my aunt and cousin in Billericay. There I saw the Essex Regiment marching up and down the road, half in army uniform and half in their own clothes. They had army trousers and their own jackets or the other way around. They could not help it but they looked a right shower!

Mary Cockie (Miss Amos)

No plumbers

During the war there were no plumbers and the pipes in our house were always getting frozen and, as kids, we all knew how to take the big key out to the front and turn off the water, then climb into the loft and mend the pipe. I've still got some of the stuff my Mum used to wrap round them.

Yvonne Wilkinson

On tick

Dad had a shop in the East End and people used to buy things on tick but after a bad night of bombing on 7 September 1940 he just shut up the shop and we moved down to my aunt's at Nevendon. When we went back to see if the shop was all right, people would say, 'I haven't forgotten how much I owe you.' My dad was a butcher but he would make a penny out of anything, he even ran bets although it was illegal. He used to be on the music hall and when the war was over he put our piano out in Wick Drive and played all night.

Val Dowman

I was stunned

My husband was a signaller and after his training was sent to Africa, but on the way out his boat was damaged and was diverted to Freetown. While he was there, the Japanese attacked Pearl Harbour and so he had to learn the Japanese codes in three months. He was sent to India and was the first into Singapore. He was then posted to Burma, where he was promoted to RSM. Dad and my uncle were in the Home Guard. We used to watch the doodlebugs going up the Thames. Rochford Council did not supply shelters but the bungalow across the road came under Billericay and they had one and so we used theirs. A rocket dropped in the orchard at twenty-five to eleven one morning in October 1944. My daughter was twelve months old at the time and she was in her pram outside the door. Luckily, it started to rain and I picked her up and brought her in. Mum had just said, 'Shall we go shopping up Shotgate?' when the rocket went off, taking the hood of the pram clean off. I was stunned and somehow cut my chin. Dad and Uncle Tom were up in the yard with a horse which jumped in the air with the shock. We were running around in circles with all the windows smashed and the roof badly damaged. We were out of the house until March and stayed with Jackie, my niece.

Joan Cox

Ted Cox in tropical uniform in Madras, India in 1944.

Battle of Britain

I was over the fields picking blackberries during the Battle of Britain. We could see the planes dive and twirl like leaves. My daughter said, 'Don't stop and look, they are only ours.' She was only a little tot. I remember standing on my doorstep and seeing a German plane with the cross underneath. I could see the pilot, who looked like he had been machine-gunned and was trying to get home. We lived in Southend Road and did not even have a window broken but were shaken sometimes when a rocket came down. Chapel Row in Runwell Road were old houses with mud floors and the roofs caved in.

Queenie Thorington

Teacher training

Until I was eighteen, I went to a grammar school in Bracknell and then, because all our relations were in Wickford, we packed up all our things and moved here. In September 1939 I should have gone to college in London but because the war had started I stayed at home and, under the college's supervision, I did a term's teaching at Billericay Secondary School. From January 1940 until the July, I went to college in London. Then in September 1940, still unqualified, I did a term in Stock Primary School. As London was being badly bombed, they sent us up to Cardiff to do our teacher training. I obtained private digs and settled back, glad to be away from the danger, but Cardiff was blasted off the face of the earth as the Germans had decided to leave London alone and bomb the ports. I did my finals in 1941 and started teaching in Wickford Secondary School in September 1941.

Mary Cockie (Miss Amos)

The first bomb

The first bomb that dropped on England fell on Wickford on 25 May 1940, behind the houses which front Southend Road and Westbeech Avenue. The locals thought it was an army shell that had misfired. Apparently, the papers got hold of the story. The first war victim in Wickford was a chicken. The yellow peril was a small bomb which killed a lot of kids, luckily not in Wickford. The Germans used a basket which burst open and scattered them everywhere, going off when somebody picked them up. In a dig in Norsey Woods we found thirty-seven incendiaries. Police Sergeant Brewer said that Norsey Woods was full of incendiary bombs.

Trevor Williams

Black Watch

Any empty property in Wickford was taken over by the Black Watch until they went over to France. One of the places they were billeted was the old baker's opposite the fish and chip shop in the High Street. Dad used to keep chickens and had a surplus of soft-shelled eggs so he put them in trays and I took them round to the soldiers. You never heard the V2 rockets but I saw one once. I was at a cricket match at the senior school and was lying down waiting to go in to bat when I saw something pass from one cloud to the next and then boom! The rocket fell over Billericay way.

Peter Hall

My mum married a soldier

My mum married one of the soldiers that were billeted in Nevendon Road. He had been a prisoner of war for five years.

Jackie Joyce

Adcock's newsagents after an air raid in 1941.

Newts and tadpoles

Bert Ford's scrapyard had bomb holes which soon filled up with water and it was not long before there were newts and tadpoles. While the Army were digging out bombs, my mum would make the soldiers cocoa and I would take it over to them.

Fred Smith

Not everyone joined up

I did not join up but looked after the Land Army girls on the farm and was a sort of messenger in the Home Guard. A bomb dropped in a field opposite the Chichester Farm and blew out all the windows. They dropped four that night; the others were dropped on Battlesbridge. A doodlebug dropped at Battlesbridge, falling on the railway cottage and making a nasty hole in a woman's stomach. An aircraft fell in Castledon Road. The pilot was blown to bits, which hung in the trees. If a German plane came back from London with any bombs left, they dropped them before they crossed the Channel. There were five or six guns in the field opposite the Carpenters' Arms. Every time they fired, they went down in the mud and they had a hell of a job to get them out.

Ernie Woods

Bombing raids

I remember sitting in the kitchen while my aunt did the greens and Chamberlain came on the radio at eleven o'clock on Sunday morning and said that a state of war existed with Germany. We always gathered round the radio when Churchill spoke because he reassured people. 1940 at Wickford Infants' School was a bad year, as we spent most of our time in the air-raid shelters. The worst nights of the whole lot were the nights of 10 and 11 May 1941, when 1,400 people were killed in London. The raids never seemed to end. On Saturday 7 September 1940 I remember my uncle looking up at the sky and saying, 'They will be coming tonight.' That night, London's dockland was set alight by 1,000 bombers and fighters and more returned later to bomb the flames. I stood in the garden at Elm Road looking towards the Thames and saw hundreds of German planes heading for London. I could see the anti-aircraft fire bursting in front of them. The Germans used to follow the Thames. I remember seeing forty German aircraft being attacked by only three RAF Hurricanes.

I remember the Highland Light Infantry coming back from Dunkirk. They stayed in the public hall and some were billeted on us. A couple of them married local girls and are still living here. We thought we could not lose the war but during the bad times, when the flying bombs were coming over, people could not handle it. We had the flying bombs about a week after D-Day. You could hear them coming and when the noise stopped, you knew it was going to nosedive and then of course we had the V2s, which you never heard. All you heard was the tremendous explosion. My wife's house was blown to bits but luckily nobody was hurt. On the radio I remember hearing that we had bombed Germany and then at the end of the broadcast they would say how many of our aircraft were missing. I remember hearing the roar of our bombers as they gathered for a raid. We slept easily in our beds the nights that Hitler attacked Russia and the Japs attacked Pearl Harbour.

I was really saddened sometimes when I got home from school and my aunt would say, 'Mrs So-and-So's son is missing. They don't hold out a lot of hope.' Most of them were in the RAF: Don Murray, Stan Pimm and Ken Gowen. They made a mistake when they bombed Nuremberg on a bright moonlit night on 31 March 1944. I remember on the radio in the kitchen hearing that ninety-five of our aircraft were missing.

I was in Wickford cinema with Ron Epson when they flashed up that the war was over. Next morning, Mr Rose the headmaster announced it in assembly. That night, all round Wickford market there were fires and normal, sensible people went mad. My aunt, who was a bit of a churchgoer, was dancing and singing away.

John Dowman

Blood transfusions

During the war Runwell Hospital treated anybody. The blood transfusion machine broke down but when a landmine dropped harmlessly in the grounds, the hospital engineer, Mr Flack, took part of it and made a new piston for the broken machine. Two landmines dropped in the hospital grounds and Runwell Hospital had its own fire brigade.

Trevor Williams

Playing tricks

When I turned eighteen, the Ministry sent me a letter and asked what I would like to do, go in the Land Army or work in a factory? I decided I would go into Marconi. They made radios and clocks for the Navy ships. They worked in gold in the shop where I worked and would hammer it, cut it and fix it together while we put the clock face on. There were three girls and sixty men and so you can imagine what went on. The men were always playing tricks. When I got there in the morning, I would go down to the ladies to change into my overalls and put my skirt in my locker. They would take it and hide it in a basket. Sometimes I tightened nuts too much and broke the heads off but the men would drill and thread them, putting in a bigger screw. One night, the hooter went at five o'clock and I ran like hell to get out before they turned the lights off. When I got home, I found my lunchbox full of nuts and bolts. If I'd been stopped, I would have been done for

The piston for the blood transfusion machine made by Mr Flack from parts of the landmine that landed in the grounds on 6 October 1943.

Mrs Reeves learning new skills at Marconi during the Second World War.

theft. Next day I heard the men talking: 'Do you know that somebody is setting up their own wireless station and is taking home nuts and bolts. The authorities are on to them!'

Mrs Reeves

A day at the seaside

We had a little Austin car but when petrol went on ration we sold it. During the war we went to Rayleigh by bus, as my husband wanted to collect his watch from the jeweller's. We got to Rawreth and the police stopped us and made me and my little girl get off because we did not have a good enough reason to travel. My husband did – his watch. We had to walk all the way back to Wickford as there were no buses. On the first day of the doodlebugs, we went to Southend by train. On the way to the station, the postman stopped us and told us about these new bombs. Down in Southend there were all obstacles on the beach but we got between them and had our picnic. The air-raid warnings went all day but we did not care, as we had a day at the seaside.

Queenie Thorington

Home Guard

The Home Guard paraded within the perimeter of the row of shops and a disused garage in Shotgate. A Home Guard sergeant, Mr Rolls, got shot and killed accidentally by a bullet which ricocheted off the front of a tractor and caught him in the eye. His grave is in St Catherine's church, next door to one of my family's. I always put flowers on it.

Yvonne Wilkinson

Ding-dongs

Wickford Home Guard used to have ding-dongs with Billericay. One would be reds and the other blues. I can remember sitting on top of the old shelter and watching them while we hit a piece of weatherboard on the roof which sounded just like a rifle. They had little flour bombs, which were imitation hand grenades, and they threw them at one another.

Peter Hall

Feet to the centre pole

I was seventeen when I joined the Home Guard. We had a spigot mortar and fired it in a field where Matalan is now. We went camping for a weekend to North Weald in this bloom-ing old Army tent, head to the wall and feet to the centre pole. I did not want to be away because I was courting at the time.

Ron Iles

The only woman in Wickford Fire Brigade

My grandfather, Samuel Wright, was in the National Fire Service and my grandmother, Ethel Wright, was the only woman in the Wickford Fire Brigade. She cooked and in her spare time worked in the soup kitchen at Wickford Congregational church, giving soup to people that were bombed out.

Trevor Williams

Called up into the RAF

In 1942 I was called up into the Royal Air Force and reported to Padgate. I did my square-bashing in Blackpool, where we would see Stanley Matthews, the footballer, doing his training at the Bloomfield Road ground. After a few weeks at Lossiemouth and a sixteen-week course at Weston-super-Mare, I was posted to Walney Island in Barrow-in-Furness, servicing Martinets which were used for towing drogues as air-gunnery targets. One day a Polish pilot got out of his aircraft and came over to look at us repairing a wing and could not believe his eyes when he saw that the wings were constructed of wooden struts. Most of my service was at Stranraer in Scotland, servicing and modifying Flying Boats.

Reg Iles

Sergeant Longman

The first war casualty from Wickford was Sergeant Leonard Longman, who died on 18 October 1940. He was killed at Yelverton on 514 Searchlight Battery. A German bomber came down the beam and before they could say 'Douse, douse, douse!', the aircraft opened up and killed the whole battery crew. He was twenty-seven years old and is buried in St Catherine's churchyard.

Trevor Williams

Wickford's first bomb victims

I was brought up more or less by my gran and grandad who lived in Jersey Gardens because my mum and dad were in the Wickford Fire Service. When my dad was on duty, my mum used to come home but would never go down the shelter. One night when I was eight, Mum and I were in the little back bedroom when the siren went off. I looked out the window and saw this great big red glow in the sky and a parachute floating across our window. Mum pushed me on the bed just as there was this terrific explosion and the windows came in.

Mum shouted, 'Quick, down the shelter!' We ran down the glass-littered stairs and when I got to the bottom I could not believe I hadn't cut my feet. The landmine landed a few hundred yards away on the Pratts' house in Swan Lane, killing them. Our roof was off but their house was gutted.

Doreen Williams

Protecting the railway bridge

My father worked for the Department of Agriculture and Fisheries in a reserved occupation. Three times he and his mate bunked off to join up but were sent back and he had to stay there right till the end of the war. My dad always treated things with a sense of humour although he took being a member of Wickford Home Guard very seriously. We used to pull one another's legs and I used to say to him, 'What were you guarding in Wickford, Dad?' He used to say with a grin, 'Never you mind, son. I was on secret war work.' It turned out he was guarding Wickford railway bridge. I asked him what he would have done if the Germans had invaded and again he smiled and said, 'There was no point in shedding blood over a bridge. I would probably have gone in the Castle pub and over a pint discussed who had rightful ownership of it.' He said that they paraded a machine gun through Wickford every weekend but what nobody knew was that they did not have any bullets.

Trevor Williams

Two brothers on parade

They did not waste any time in calling me up: I was eighteen on the second of July, had my medical on the fifth, my call-up papers on the fifteenth and I was in the Army on the twentieth. I could not believe it but my brother, who is fifteen years older than me, was called up on the same day and we went to the same place.

He had been in a reserved occupation. I think why they wanted us was because they were short of troops after D-Day. I stayed at my brother's in Watford on the Tuesday night and then we travelled up to Blackpool on our rail warrants. We did not stay together. He was a big strong bloke and I was underweight. I was only there a fortnight when they sent me to a Physical Development Centre for eight weeks' physical training. The fellows used to joke about my weight and say that when I turned sideways they could not see me. There were so many jokes about me, like they did not know if it was two rifles standing on parade or they could use me for a flagpole.

After I finished that, they sent me to Bradford for six weeks' basic training and then to

Mr Reeves in his Army uniform.

Norwich, where I did my battalion stint. I was in the Dorset Regiment in Nelson Barracks. On 31 July 1945 we were posted to Malaya. We were in the middle of the Indian Ocean when it was announced that the Japanese war was over. A loud cheer went up. We were so relieved. If I remember rightly, they issued us some beer to celebrate. So instead of doing jungle training when we landed in Bombay, we got transferred to the First Battalion of the Devonshire Regiment. We stayed in India for four months and then just before Christmas 1945 we were transferred to Singapore. I had eighteen months in Malaya and guarded Changi prison. Unfortunately, my father died and they flew me back home in a Yorkie. When I got home I received a certificate and thirty bob from the people of Wickford. They gave them to all returning soldiers to thank them for their war efforts.

Mr Reeves

Evacuees from London

I was in the garden with my mother when the roadsweeper, Mr Crow, said, 'I've just heard that war has been declared.' Soon after, we had evacuees coming down from London. They were distributed out among the people and went to school in the mornings and we went in the afternoons. The next week it would be the other way around. After a while, because there were no raids, the evacuees started to dwindle home. Most food was on ration and you could not have sausages if you had liver.

Mrs Reeves

Japan's surrender

By 1944 most of my mates were in the forces and so at seventeen and a half I volunteered for the Royal Navy. A lot of the activity had finished by that time. After training, I sailed out to Sydney, Australia, where we were pre-

paring a large camp to house the soldiers for the invasion of Japan. Fortunately, that never happened because the Japanese surrendered after the atomic bomb.

Norman Simmons

Chased by a submarine

I was in the Merchant Navy and was two weeks from home when on 3 September 1939, as we gathered round the ship's radio, we heard Chamberlain declare that we were at war. It was a horrible feeling. We wondered if we were going to get home all right, as we were aware that the German submarines were waiting for us. I was a trimmer at first, running the coal for the boiler. Then I got made up to a fireman and fed the boilers. Two men jumped ship and as a result I got promoted to the engine room as a greaser and had to keep the engines cool and the lights going. I did twelve hours on and twenty-four hours off. We were near Montreal, Canada in the ship SS *Materoa* when a German submarine came up. We had a gun and were going to fire but the captain shouted, 'No, leave it! We'll make a run for it!' We opened up full speed. Looking out, we were terrified to see it was still following us, then suddenly it disappeared. We prayed that it had given up but we still kept a lookout and then, after a while, we all breathed a sigh of relief when we realised it had gone. When the war ended I was on my way back from Canada to Glasgow.

Mr Spindler

Silver paper

We went into the fields looking for silver paper, which was dropped by the Germans to confuse the radar. If the air-raid warning went off and we were eating, we got our food and went straight down the air-raid shelter. At first, when the siren went off my mother would go into the garden and pick up corrugated sheets and lay them over the kitchen table and all seven of us would get underneath but there was not enough room for her. We got bombed out in London and I had one of those gas masks that they put babies in. My gran put me in it and ran out of the house, leaving everybody behind.

Mrs Livermore

Prisoners of war

They had an Italian prisoner-of-war camp over near Rayleigh and when I went out with my brothers and sisters, we sometimes walked along the railway tracks where the Italian prisoners were working. They would call out after us but we never looked round.

Yvonne Wilkinson

German prisoners

The camp near Makro was at first an English Army camp and I remember them marching up to Rawreth church every Sunday for a church parade. Later, they turned it into a German prisoner-of-war camp. There were some good blokes among the Germans. One of them became the foreman at Garden Beauty Products and then after the war he took over. He came to me in the end – I was the one who dug his grave.

Ernie Woods

They did not want to escape

We had an Italian prisoner-of-war camp up Nevendon Road, where the bungalows are up on the left. They had wooden huts. The Italians did not want to escape. They were nice people. They helped to build the prefabs. We used to go up an old crab apple tree and throw crab apples at them. A lot of the prisoners worked on the farms. After the war, one

of these Germans became a blacksmith and married an English girl.

Peter Hall

I decided to stay

I was captured towards the end of the war in Germany. My friend and I were separated from our unit and we sat on a hill looking down on the American tanks. If we went one way, there were the Russians so we decided to surrender to the Americans. They first took us to America and then for some unknown reason they shipped us to England and I finished up near Rayleigh. We worked on the farms round here. I cannot remember their names but they were good to us and at the end of the war we had a lot of freedom. I used to swim in the river and got talking to my future brother-in-law, who invited me back to his place for tea and that is how I met my wife. I decided to stay in England, where I worked for a number of farms.

Carl Beck

Friendly alien

I was brought up in Germany and came to England when I was sixteen, in 1939, just nine days before the outbreak of the war. At first, I was put in a hostel in London and then moved to Cliftonville, Margate. Then the war broke out and I can remember hearing Neville Chamberlain's speech. I was very frightened and wondered what was going to happen. I did not have long to wait, as I was called in front of a committee of twelve honourable citizens who sat round a horseshoe table. They asked if I wanted to go back to Germany. When I said no, they registered me as a friendly alien and I got a registration book.

I wanted to work and so returned to Finchley Road in London, where I went to the Labour Exchange. They told me there was no work but if I did find any I must tell them. When I found a job, I told them and they gave the job to an English boy, as they came first. I found a number of good jobs but they were snapped up the same. Finally I got a job in a boarding house, working eighty-seven hours a week for seven shillings and sixpence. Nobody else wanted it. I did that for a year and then the Blitz started and the docks were bombed. My employer expressed concern for my safety, as I was sleeping at the top of the house, and told me I could sleep in the basement. She then promptly let my room. I then got a job in a factory near Regents Park, which was owed by a Polish Jew. He made Army uniforms and I earned twenty-five shillings a week, working only forty-eight hours.

I did fire-watching after work, then on 19 June 1941 I heard my parents had been deported to a concentration camp and had possibly been killed. I wanted to do something to help the war effort so I volunteered to join the Army. At first, I was only allowed to join the Pioneers but then, in 1943, I learned that Germans and other foreigners could join a fighting unit and so I volunteered for the Tank Corps. I was advised to change my name from Karl Worzburger in case I got captured and so I chose Ward. The only trouble was that my dogtag had my religion on it, 'J' for Jew. I knew if I got captured I would have to get rid of it. I landed on Gold Beach in Normandy on D-Day, as a wireless operator in a Firefly tank in the 1st Royal Tank Regiment. The Firefly tank had a special gun. I went through the war and survived four tanks. When the war finished, I was transferred to the interpreters' pool and attached to the Military Police in Berlin.

Ken Ward

Ken Ward back in Germany.

Carter and Ward

When my husband came out of the Army, Carter and Ward, the builders, were waiting for him to take charge of a lot of the prisoners of war who were repairing roads and buildings. One of the prisoners made wooden brown-and-black spot-ted dogs with wiggly tails for the children. They made several things for them. I think it was because my husband was quite decent to them. My husband was a bricklayer but because of the war a man taught him civil engineering. He told people what to do but would not ask anybody to do anything that he could not do himself.

Queenie Thorington

They carried me on their shoulders

My father had a couple of prisoners of war working on his farm and they used to carry me on their shoulders. One of them could not wait to go back and the other one wanted to stay.

Anne Goddard

Ken Ward and his crew on their tank.

A fireman holding up an incendiary bomb, 1940.

When the evacuees came

When the evacuees came down, they moved into the prefabs up Nevendon Road. The school had a collection for them and, although none of us was well off, we took clothes and blankets in for them.

Yvonne Wilkinson

Evacuated to Ipswich

At fourteen I was evacuated with my two sisters to Ipswich but there was no organisation and I was taken in by a Mrs Green and my two sisters were lodged one and a half miles away. On the first night, there was a heavy raid but I was not afraid, in fact we thought it was quite an adventure. After six months, my father's firm moved to Cambridge and so we followed our parents.

Norman Simmons

That was the last I saw of him

Under the War Agricultural Ministry, we cultivated all the land round Wickford. I was attached to Lynford's Farm, in Runwell Road opposite the café. There was one boy who lived next door to the café, in the cycle shop. He was twenty-one when he went into the RAF. He was a nice bloke. He worked at Rushbrooks Farm, up Runwell Road. I shook hands with him and that was the last I saw of him. He was a rear gunner in a Lancaster and his plane bellyflopped and exploded. He is buried in Runwell churchyard.

One day I went into the pub for my lunch, leaving the tractor outside. I came out at two o'clock and was talking to Harry Ledge and an old bloke who used to do the hedges and ditches. Suddenly there was this whistling sound and we all dived for the ditch. The bomb came right over the top of us and then we heard a thud but it did not go off and is still there today. It is in one of the fields at the back of Runwell Hospital.

During the early part of the war, I was working at Lynfords Farm and had just turned the corner when I saw nine Fokke Wulfs hedge-hopping. I was so astounded I just stood there transfixed and counted them. I could see the pilots and the swastikas on the sides. That is when they went over and bombed Ilford. The story was that our boys caught the raiders as they flew back.

Another time, I was working on a tractor in a field in Church End Lane, getting the potatoes out. I had four or five Land Girls working with me and it was very foggy, then right above us we heard droning and about fifty yards above there was a German plane, I could see the crosses on it. I could have hit it with a stone. He looked as if he did not know how close he was to the ground nor where he was. He turned the plane on its side and went up over some trees . I don't know how he missed them.

Mr Williams Senior

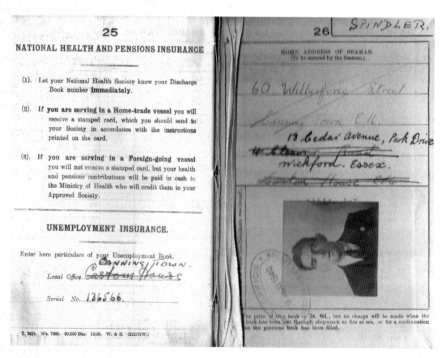

Left: Mr Spindler's Continuous Certificate Of Discharge from the Merchant Navy, 1940.

Opposite: A dinner in 1940, possibly for the Home Guard.

Got any gum, chum?

During the war, there was a big American base just outside Chelmsford. Occasionally we visited an aunt in Chelmsford and, when passing the Yanks in the street, the familiar saying was: 'Got any gum, chum?' They usually obliged.

Peter Hall

Nothing I could do

I was in Australia in 1944 with the Merchant Navy when I had a telegram telling me my mother had died. She was only sixty-eight and died because she did not get enough food. She gave it all to my father. She was starving herself to make sure he was all right. There was nothing I could do.

Mr Spindler

Doodlebugs and V2s

We had one of the first doodlebugs near here, in Borwick Lane. My mum got up and looked out the window and thought it had been shot down because the engine had stopped. The next thing she knew was that she was thrown back on the bed. It must have dropped a good half-mile away. We also had a V2 drop, which took the roof off. It happened at night while we were fast asleep. There was a sudden crash and I jumped up. I remember the falling rubble. The walls were asbestos and collapsed. All the windows were broken on the side the bomb landed but luckily the glass embedded itself into the wall and did not come through. The old manor house up the road is sixteenth century and when the rocket dropped on the other side of the road it did not do much damage.

Stan Gregory

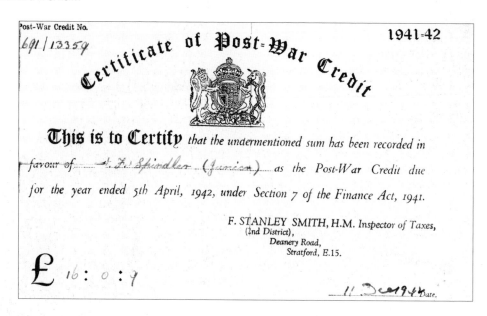

A Certificate of Post-War Credit awarded to Mr Spindler for 1941-42.

Potatoes down my boots

I was in the Land Army at sixteen and worked on most of the farms round here. We picked potatoes and peas and harvested, stacking up the sheaves of corn. When the potatoes came out, I had an old sack round me and I used to put some potatoes down my boots to help out at home. The old foreman used to look at me because I was limping but never said anything. In winter we cut down hedges, it was freezing. We used to wear a uniform. We were working near the Harrow pub, right out in the open fields, and an old boy who lived in an old cottage came out and shouted, 'The war's over!' The foreman shouted out, 'Get on with your work. You'll have tomorrow off!'.

Emily Babbage

End of hostilities

After the war we had a big party and I was a beauty queen. Well, to tell the truth, there were about four of us. We were all picked as we were part of the dancing troupe. We had another party when Ron Smith came home from the Japanese prisoner-of-war camp a long time after the war finished. He was so thin and ill. He looked like a yellow skeleton. They had to keep him in hospital for a long time.

Yvonne Wilkinson

An early demob

In May 1945 I was transferred to the Royal Navy Fleet Air Arm for the Far East Campaign but the bombing of Hiroshima and Nagasaki rendered the transfer superfluous, giving me an early demob grouping and I was discharged in March 1946 from HMS *Gadwall*. I was issued with a nice suit and I brought home my toolbox and hammock. A year before I was demobbed I married my wife, a Wickford lass. Chas Scott, a schoolfriend, neighbour and Home Guard colleague, was my best man. We are both widowers now and we share the driving when we go bowling.

Reg Iles

Above: A Victory street party in Wickford at the end of the Second World War.

Right: Ron Smith in uniform, 1945.

Jelly and custard

At the end of the war, they held big street parties. In Runwell Road the party stretched right along. There were flags all over the place. Everybody did something. Jelly and custard, sandwiches and jam tarts.

Mrs Livermore

Homecoming

I remember the lads coming home and the reception they had in Raweth Parish Hall with the corrugated roof. Frankie Howerd came and entertained them.

Mrs Barker

Shipped out to India

In 1945/46 I was called up and went in the Air Force and after my training I was shipped out to India. I was out there when Gandhi was shot in 1947. I was very fortunate, as I was on tour with Lord Mountbatten. Then India became independent in August 1947 and all hell let loose, Hindus and Muslims fought one another and then of course the country was divided between India and Pakistan. I was out there for another year on a staging post at Karachi and was demobbed in late 1948, when I went back into the family business.

Roy Hall

National Service

Birthday present

In 1949 I got called up for National Service. I had been in the ATC and got called up on my dad's birthday and he reckoned that was the best birthday present he had ever had.

Peter Hall

The Coronation procession

After my apprenticeship, I went in the Army for my National Service. I was in there two weeks and got sent to the Worcestershire Regiment. I went to the sergeant major's office and was informed that I was on the Coronation parade on 2 June 1953. I was sent to Malvern in Worcestershire, No. 1 Training Regiment. I trained by marching to places like Upton-on-Severn and then came the great day. We moved down to Aldershot for a week and the area was all marked out just like the real parade, with tapes and chalk. All those marching in the procession were moved into the car park at Earls Court and those that lined the route were under canvas in Kensington Gardens. On the day, I was marching in the Coronation procession with my blue uniform and white belt but unfortunately it started to pour down and all our blanco started to run down our uniforms. We were in a real state waiting while the Queen was crowned in Westminster Abbey.

I was drafted to Korea and spent six weeks in Japan. When I was out east, somebody tapped me on the shoulder – it was Roy Carter. I used to work for his old man as an apprentice. Ironically, I was a corporal and he was a private. When I got back to England I was a bricklayer and he was a managing director. I was lucky, as I just missed the Korean War by two months.

John Dowman

I volunteered for aircrew

I was called up for National Service in 1952 and signed on for four years in the Air Force. I volunteered for aircrew and trained as a navigator in Canada. After qualifying, I was posted to Coastal Command at St Mawgan, Cornwall for maritime reconnaisance training. The course was reputed to be one of the hardest in the RAF. We flew in Lancasters and, incidentally, St Mawgan was the last RAF unit to operate with this legendary aircraft. I was then posted to RAF Kinloss in Scotland to convert to Shackletons and then back to St Ivel in Cornwall, where I joined 228 Squadron, also flying Shackletons.

Charles Read

eight
Transport

It was so uncomfortable

There was an old bus run by Campbell's. It had wooden seats and when you went round corners you went flying. It was so uncomfortable.

Emily Babbage

Shotgate Flyer

There used to be a bus through here that we called the Shotgate Flyer. It ran solely from Shotgate to Wickford and back. One of the drivers I talked to years later on the CB radio said that he remembered taking me to school on his bus because I was a little bugger.

Fred Smith

They laid straw on the road

In 1920, when I was about ten, everyone went around in pony-and-traps. One of my aunts was very ill with cancer and they laid straw down on the road outside her home to deaden the sound of the horses' hooves.

Queenie Thorington

Just like charabancs

I remember the Campbell's single-decker buses, they were just like charabancs. You could set your alarm clock by them. They had female clippies. There used also to be the No. 151 and the No. 251. They came from Wood Green, through Brentwood and down to Southend. The only thing they would not allow you to do was to take an accumulator on board, in case you spilt the acid. They were big batteries for the wireless. So I had to carry them in a big cardboard box tied up with string to the garage in Wickford to get them charged and once done you had to go back and get them and then carry them all the way home again.

Yvonne Wilkinson

Campbell's coach on its run to Pitsea.

A pony-and-trap in contrast with an early car outside the Swan, 1938.

Aircraft factory

During the First World War, my Uncle Will worked at an aircraft factory at Wembley, making wires for the fuselage of the Camel and Dolphin planes. He travelled up there from Wickford on a 1913 Triumph motor-bike.

Joan Blackburn

I walked everywhere

When I was a kid, I had nothing to get about with and so I walked. I walked to Rayleigh one day. I walked up Crown Hill and stood there with Rayleigh High Street spread out before me. It's nothing like that today.

Ernie Woods

Coal was brought on a mud sledge

In 1926, when I was three years old, we moved into Ozonia Road. All our furniture was brought down by horse and cart from Paddington in London and we arrived in Wickford in the early hours of the morning. My brother Jim was still in the forces and my other brother worked on the railway. In those days, all the roads were higgledy-piggledy. Elder Avenue was a tree-lined mud track. In the winter, any coal delivered by Warner's was brought down on a mud sledge.

We then moved to North Benfleet, where we had big oil lamps. The problem was that when you sat at the table to read, you had to get in the circle of light. Then Dad had gas installed and so we had gas mantles, which were not all that brilliant but it was better than going up to bed with a candle or little old oil lamp. When you

A lone cyclist outside Upson's in the early 1900s.

entered the back door, you were straight into the scullery and there, in the corner, stood the big copper. All the hot water was boiled up in it for baths and so on and we all bathed in the same water. Mum cooked on a big range and the big old stew pot steamed away. I used to look after the pigs on my dad's smallholding.

Mr Nightingale

I saw him fly up in the air

One of the Campbell's buses used to pull up outside our shop every afternoon. One day, I was looking out the window of the shop and suddenly I saw this bloke fly right up in the air, hitting our shop window. He had begun to crank up the bus to start it and it had kicked back and broke his arm.

Barrie Adcock

On the buses

My dad worked on the horse buses up in London before coming to Wickford.

Mr Reeves

You could always get a seat

I was born in Kentish Town and moved to Wickford in 1961 because my daughter suffered from asthma. Wickford had a good railway line up to London, which was reliable, ran on time and you could always get a seat. When I went to visit my relations, the connections for the Southminster train were sometimes awkward. They had steam trains in those days going to Southend.

Doreen Reed

Stoking up the boiler

When I was young, I used to help stoke up the boiler on the branch line steam train. I was not supposed to but I went out as far as Woodham Ferrers. The line went to Southminster and Latchingdon. My mother said she never saw me from one week's end to the next.

Barrie Adcock

Mr Reeves' father with a horse bus in the early 1900s.

Wickford High Street, 1950s. Note the old car and bus.

The High Street in the mid-1950s, practically empty except for a single Ford Popular.

Woolshots farm milk lorry, driven by Jack Humphries.

nine

Famous and Infamous People of Wickford

One in a million

My husband, Dr Charles Pocock MBE, was born in the small mining village of Landybie, South Wales in 1924. He suffered from a very rare congenital disability called diastrophic dysphasia, which apparently occurs in approximately one in a million births, hence the title of his book, *One in a Million*. Despite his enormous physical difficulties, he was a great inspiration to so many people throughout his life. I was born in Wales and Charles and I met when he visited my church as a lay preacher.

In the early days, Charles worked for an agricultural college but could see his prospects were limited and so he applied for the post of General Secretary with the Disabled Drivers' Association, which necessitated a move from Wales to Wickford in 1963. After a number of years, he became Public Relations Manager for Remploy Ltd, which meant him travelling a great deal to and from their ninety-seven factories across the British Isles. Despite his disability and lack of education – much of his childhood was spent in hospital – he was a gifted public speaker and was often invited to give lectures.

Charles did much for, and on behalf of, disabled people and was involved with the introduction of the Orange Badge Scheme, now Blue Badge. He worked closely with Lord Alfred Morris to implement the 1970 Chronically Sick and Disabled Persons Act. He appeared in a film directed by Lord Snowdon regarding the problems of restricted growth, entitled *Born to be Small*. He also did a number of television and radio interviews over the years. He was instrumental in founding the Restrictive Growth Association; he later became their president. During the International Year of the Disabled in 1981, we were privileged to attend a garden party at Buckingham Palace and were able to talk with the Queen and other members of the Royal Family. In 1985 Charles was awarded the MBE. He also received an Honorary Doctorate at the University of Regina in Canada. In 1997 he received the Lord Snowdon Award and attended the House of Lords, where he spoke.

Locally he was involved in committee work, including the Wickford Area Committee and the Essex Physically Handicapped Association. He was also governor of Kingsdown School in Southend. Just before he died, he wrote his autobiography, which I had published. He was a wonderful person and it was a privilege to have been married to such a wonderful person who helped so many.

Barbara Pocock

Alvin Stardust

Alvin Stardust is a pop star whose mother

Dr Charles Pocock MBE with his family.

had a café up near the station. The café had photographs of Alvin on the walls. He used to dress up in outlandish, brightly coloured clothes. I did not like his music and never saw him at the café but I was told he did go there sometimes.

Joan Blackburn

Picture shows
I did my very first show at Rawreth for the man who used to have the Heron Stables. He asked if I would do a show there to help raise funds for a new hall to replace the old tin hut. Since my book, *Wickford* in the *Archive Photographs Series* was published, I have put together a slide show on Wickford and have done over 200 shows for various organisations and schools in the district.

Peter Hall

Local historian Barrie Adcock today.

He was a street bookie
We used to have an old boy called Harry come down from the station. He used to be a street bookie, which was illegal, and he would walk up to the station to pick up the newspapers for our shop on a Saturday night and by the time he came down he had practically sold all of them and paid out most of the winning bets.

Barrie Adcock

A goose waddling behind him
There used to be a man who was in the Salvation Army and he would go down the High Street with a great big English dog and a goose waddling behind him.

Emily Babbage

He had quite a few lions
Billy Foyle used to come to our carnival on his horse, dressed up like a cowboy, and had this place down Crays Hill which was a miniature zoo. He had quite a few lions, which you could hear roaring miles away. People used to get very worried about it.

Barrie Adcock

What murder?
Mr Fitt used to be the reporter for the *Wickford Times*. He walked in the shop one day and my father looked up and asked, 'Ralph, have you been up and reported the murder?' Mr Fitt looked puzzled and said, 'Murder, what murder?' My father replied, 'It's in all the daily papers, a Mr Howard has murdered his wife!' I understand it was the second murder in the house. This was sometime in the fifties or sixties.

Barrie Adcock

Other local titles published by Tempus

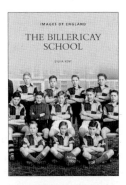

The Billericay School
SYLVIA KENT

The creation of the Billericay School in 1937 as the town's first senior school marked the beginning of an exciting new era for the town and its families. This collection of over 200 photographs presents a unique pictorial record of the history of the school and its forerunner, the Great Burstead Board School. This book chronicles some of the changes and events for all those involved: teachers, parents, and pupils.

0 7524 3083 1

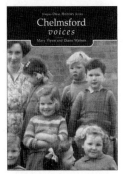

Chelmsford Voices
MARY FLYNN AND DIANE WATSON

This book records the reminiscences of Chelmsford's inhabitants in their own words, accompanied throughout by an intriguing selection of photographs, many drawn from the family albums of the contributors themselves. The memories range through all aspects of the town's life, from home and school life to the workplace, shops and their proprietors, and leisure pursuits.

0 7524 2202 2

Southend Voices
FRANCES CLAMP

This book brings together the personal memories of people who have lived and grown up in the seaside town of Southend-on-Sea during the last century. Reminiscences range from childhood games, working days and memories of the war years, to schools, churches and some of the local characters. The stories are complemented by over 120 photographs drawn from the private collections of the contributors.

0 7524 3215 X

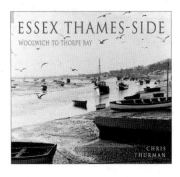

Essex Thames-side: Woolwich to Thorpe Bay
CHRIS THURMAN

This volume takes a tour of the Thames from Woolwich to Thorpe Bay on the Essex side of the river. From the futuristic sight of the Thames Barrier to sleepy Thorpe Bay, from unloading in the docks at Tilbury to cockling at Leigh on Sea, from Dagenham to Southend, the changing landscape of Essex Thames-side is photographed over the past forty years in this stunning collection of images.

0 7524 3232 X

If you are interested in purchasing other books published by Tempus, or in case you have difficulty finding any Tempus books in your local bookshop, you can also place orders directly through our website

www.tempus-publishing.com